EINSTEIN'S
BOSS

ROBERT HROMAS
with Christopher Hromas

10 RULES FOR LEADING GENIUS

EINSTEIN'S
BOSS

AMERICAN MANAGEMENT ASSOCIATION

New York • Atlanta • Brussels • Chicago • Mexico City • San Francisco
Shanghai • Tokyo • Toronto • Washington, D.C.

Bulk discounts available. For details visit:
www.amacombooks.org/go/specialsales
Or contact special sales:
Phone: 800-250-5308
Email: specialsls@amanet.org
View all the AMACOM titles at: www.amacombooks.org
American Management Association: www.amanet.org

This publication is designed to provide accurate and authoritative information in regard to the subject matter covered. It is sold with the understanding that the publisher is not engaged in rendering legal, accounting, or other professional service. If legal advice or other expert assistance is required, the services of a competent professional person should be sought.

Library of Congress Cataloging-in-Publication Data

Names: Hromas, Robert, author. | Hromas, Christopher, author.
Title: Einstein's boss : 10 rules for leading genius / Robert Hromas with
   Christopher Hromas.
Description: New York : AMACOM, [2018] | Includes bibliographical references
   and index.
Identifiers: LCCN 2017055428 (print) | LCCN 2018005509 (ebook) | ISBN
   9780814439333 (ebook) | ISBN 9780814439326 (hardcover)
Subjects: LCSH: Personnel management. | Communication in management. |
   Ability.
Classification: LCC HF5549 (ebook) | LCC HF5549 .H726 2018 (print) | DDC
   658.3--dc23
LC record available at https://lccn.loc.gov/2017055428

Illustrations by Adrian Avram

About AMA

American Management Association (www.amanet.org) is a world leader in talent development, advancing the skills of individuals to drive business success. Our mission is to support the goals of individuals and organizations through a complete range of products and services, including classroom and virtual seminars, webcasts, webinars, podcasts, conferences, corporate and government solutions, business books, and research. AMA's approach to improving performance combines experiential learning—learning through doing—with opportunities for ongoing professional growth at every step of one's career journey.

10 9 8 7 6 5 4 3 2 1

We dedicate this book to Shari Hromas,
who believed in it before anyone else,
and to Gabrielle Hromas, whose steadfast
support inspired its completion.

CONTENTS

A NOTE FROM THE AUTHOR

I wish I had this book when I took my first leadership position. I went in blind and made many mistakes that I regret. As a leukemia specialist and the dean at the Lozano Long School of Medicine at University of Texas Health Center at San Antonio, I lead a medical school with more than 1,300 faculty, 900 medical students, nearly 3,000 staff, and over 800 physicians in training. In addition, I supervise a laboratory that designs new cancer drugs. In my previous position as chair of the Department of Medicine at the University of Florida, I am proud to say that the department spun off more than $1 billion in biotechnology transfer.

I have to lead experts in many disciplines, including organic chemists, molecular biologists, interventional cardiologists, and laser-wielding dermatologists. From biomedical engineers to mathematicians, from physiologists to molecular pharmacologists, I also manage hundreds of scientists who are not physicians. We support a diverse group of computer scientists, including hardware builders, software programmers, cyber-security experts, and information analysts. Our team includes journalists, quality experts, psychologists, marketers, accountants, and MBAs working in central administration. My experience with all these very smart professionals has taught me that genius does not come in one size or shape, nor is it found more in one job than another. Hundreds of people with the spark of genius, expert in a variety of disciplines, are members of our team. What I know for certain is that this impressive group of geniuses demands new Rules for leadership.

My challenges involve managing genius in a wide range of different fields within a single organization, implementing advances into practice, and managing meaningful outcomes. The most difficult aspect of my job is getting all the brilliant people on my team to work together. Most geniuses think they know best what is needed and tend to go in their own directions, which can mean that nothing gets accomplished. I know from experience that managing genius is different and more complicated than other types of leadership. The upside is that if you can get geniuses to work well together, you can change the world.

"Leading geniuses is like leading an army of generals," Bob Leverence, a physician and hospital quality expert, observed. I can vouch for that. Geniuses have great insights that no one else sees, can think original thoughts, and are used to going their own way.

To be that creative, a genius must be comfortable with being alone in her or his own mind. The brilliant computer scientists, physicians, and molecular biologists in my department do not like to think that I am leading them. They like to function independently of me and of one another. Throughout history, geniuses made their great advances in the solitude of their own minds.

Today, technology is driving successful organizations. Economist Robert Solow won a Nobel Prize for recognizing that every major economic expansion comes not so much from expanding labor or infrastructure but from advancing technology. This engine of economic expansion is known as the Solow Residual. Growth in infrastructure and labor account for only 15 percent of the growth in U.S. economic output. The Solow Residual makes up the rest, a remarkable 85 percent of U.S. economic growth.

Technological innovation requires very smart people. Those who advance technology can go past the ends of knowledge. They do not just peer over the edge, they jump off. In the past, the smartest people were at universities, but now many, if not most, of the top scientists and engineers work in publicly traded companies that make the most innovative products and drive economic expansion. Engineering, computing, and biomedical science are innovating at such an accelerated rate that even recent technologies have become obsolete. If you are not already inventing the next new thing, you are going extinct. With today's huge advances in technology, effectively leading genius is essential for productivity in this competitive environment.

Making technological advances requires that many geniuses work together, because most technology has too many moving parts and requires mastery of many distinct fields. Advances require expertise in too many areas to be made by only one individual. The problem is that most geniuses are not naturally team players. Often, their intelligence has made them loners since early childhood. They like to attack a problem their own way, on their own schedules.

Bill Gates and Elon Musk are iconic and highly visible leaders of technological innovation. Both are geniuses and leaders, but they are the exception. In general, we rarely hear about most leaders of high technology projects, because they are not making the discoveries. Leaders of genius do not win Nobel Prizes, they do not earn patents, and they are not presenting the breakthroughs in speeches at conferences. They are behind the curtain, while the genius is at the podium accepting applause.

Although genius captures the public's attention, leading geniuses is just as important to achieve technological advances. Genius alone is not enough for success. A strong leader makes the work possible by focusing the group, minimizing barriers, seeing the goal, getting others to share the vision, and deciding on the best application of a new discovery.

I have learned many things about leading geniuses by trial and error over decades. I wish I had been better prepared for some difficult and disappointing situations I faced during my career. None of the management courses I have taken have touched on the subject of leading brilliant people. I have found that commonly accepted leadership tenets often do not apply when it comes to managing the exceptionally intelligent. Having worked on both sides of the equation, as a manager and as a member of a scientific research team, I have a unique perspective on the issues that can arise and the leadership tools required to lead genius successfully. I have distilled the lessons I learned into ten practical Rules, which I implemented and tested for many years. We have written *Einstein's Boss* to expand on these Rules.

Over the years, when I faced challenging leadership situations, I wondered what it must have been like to be Einstein's boss, to be responsible for leading a man recognized to be the foremost genius of his time. I discovered that the founder of the Institute for Advanced Study in Princeton, New Jersey, Abraham Flexner, managed an entire team of internationally renowned geniuses using many of the ten Rules I devised. *Einstein's Boss* is the product of my experience, grounded with examples of innovation, success, missed opportunities, and failure in the business world, interwoven with the story of Abraham Flexner's remarkable vision and ability to get the most from the geniuses with whom he worked. When you put my Ten Rules for Leading Genius into practice, you will see creativity and productivity increase dramatically. These strategies have worked for me, and I know they will make you a more effective leader.

Einstein's Boss will give you an understanding of the complexities of leading genius, insights that will help you avoid alienating the brilliant individuals on your team, strategies for fostering teamwork and shared purpose, and guidelines for implementing my ten Rules.

—Robert Hromas, MD

EINSTEIN'S BOSS

Chances are you have no idea who Einstein's boss was. When Einstein came to
the United States to work, he reported to
Abraham Flexner. Flexner was a great ad-
ministrator, but not a genius. He started
out as a high school teacher. He did not
have a Ph.D. He was not a physicist, nor
was he a mathematician. He never wrote
a single academic paper.

   Albert Einstein was one of Flexner's
first hires at the Institute for Advanced
Studies (IAS) at Princeton University.
Einstein gave the new research center
instant credibility. Without Flexner, Einstein would not have been
at the Institute, and without Einstein, the IAS would probably
have flopped. Flexner allowed Einstein to be the public face of the
Institute for Advanced Studies during the 1930s and '40s. Flexner
was not as smart as Einstein, and he knew it, an important attri-
bute when dealing with genius. Being ruthless in his self-assessment
helped Flexner build a successful team. A dozen other extraordinary

mathematicians and physicists soon came on board, and Flexner was able to mold them into a cohesive team.

The IAS became home to thirty-three Nobel laureates, thirty-eight Field medalists for the best mathematician in the United States, and many winners of the Wolf and MacArthur prizes. The team of geniuses, which Flexner assembled, produced some of the greatest scientific advances of the twentieth century. The Institute gave the brilliant scientists freedom to be creative, but someone had to make sure everyone was paid, the place was heated in the winter, and the lights turned on, and that such a diverse group of geniuses could work together as a team to achieve specific goals. That person was Abraham Flexner, Einstein's boss. Flexner built the Institute for Advanced Studies into one of the greatest, extraordinarily productive scientific groups of all time.

Insisting that people came before brick and mortar, he was generous to the people who worked with him. He invested his capital in providing the highest salaries of the time and tenure for life without teaching responsibilities, so that the scientists at the Institute were free to spend their time on research.

He risked a lot for his scientists. He set up pensions for the faculty, which was unheard of during the Great Depression. He was betting that the economy would turn around before the pensions came due. When the first pensions needed to be paid, his endowment had trouble coming up with the monthly checks. To remedy the shortfall, he went out on the dinner circuit and generated philanthropic gifts to cover the pensions.

He was compassionate and patient, almost to a fault. Hitler was coming to power when Flexner was forming his team. He offered a position to the German physicist Hermann Weyl, who had a Jewish wife. Weyl turned down Flexner's offer, choosing to stay in his native Germany. When Hitler began his systematic destruction of Jewish life there, Weyl realized he had made a terrible mistake. Flexner reiterated his offer to Weyl, and Weyl and his wife fled Germany, joining Einstein at the IAS. Flexner met Weyl where he was at emotionally, and provided what Weyl needed even after he had rejected him.

Flexner recognized that individual motivations were different and tailored his recruiting to individual geniuses. Another IAS recruit, the innovative economist Edward Earle, suffered from tuberculosis. Flexner considered Earle a brilliant economist and a person of high character. He offered Earle a post at the IAS when no other university would touch him, because he was so ill. It took Earle years to recover, but when he did, Earle joined Einstein and Weyl. He worked hard to produce advances in economics, because he was grateful for the opportunity. Earle often mediated clashes among the complex and occasionally irascible personalities of the geniuses at the IAS. The compassion Flexner showed during Earle's health crisis led to his gratitude and loyalty.

Flexner focused on the core missions of mathematics and physics when he started the IAS. He later added economics and history. Even today there are only four departments at the IAS—math, historical studies, social science, and natural sciences. He wanted to be world class at a few things, rather than good at many things.

This focused approach is a crucial step to innovation, as advances come at the extremes of knowledge, not in the common middle, where everyone knows what you know. The key to innovation is to dig wells, not plow fields. A chemist once told me that if I wanted to get past a dense problem, I needed to narrow my focus.

Flexner created a flow of enormous talent visiting the IAS to interact with the faculty there and to review their work. He wanted fresh minds coming and going, so that the permanent faculty never became stale or complacent. Among the consulting scientists he hired were the Nobelists Niels Bohr, John von Neumann, and Paul Dirac.

Flexner was unafraid to support new approaches to old problems. He encouraged entirely new fields in which the questions had not yet been formed. He threw together physicists, economists, mathematicians, historians, and archaeologists in the hope that they would stimulate one another to greatness, and they did. For example, when the brilliant physicist John von Neumann, who joined the team permanently after visiting, became fascinated by early computers, he built one in the basement of his office building. Flexner did not remind him that he was a theoretical physicist and not an electrician playing with vacuum tubes. He let von Neumann tinker with his project, and the result was the first computer with memory storage.

In the early years of the IAS, Flexner consulted the faculty on all major decisions, especially hires, because he was not a scientist himself and valued the opinions of his team. He had regular faculty meetings at which new directions were discussed and difficulties aired. He was accessible and knew how to listen.

Flexner modeled the culture he wanted, which was a meritocracy. Achievement and not social standing defined academic rank. He broke many social barriers, hiring the best and the brightest regardless of their background. Many of the faculty were Jewish at a time when anti-Semitism was rampant at American universities. There were written quotas for admission of Jewish students into Princeton and an unspoken quota for the number of Jewish faculty. He ignored the quota system as well as the gender barrier. He hired archaeologist Hetty Goldman to a tenured position at a time when hiring women to tenured faculty positions was not done.

He put together a remarkable team of brilliant people, because he did not let preconceived concepts of propriety get in the way. He was generous, hired the smartest person regardless of social convention, and created an environment that provided freedom from defined metrics for creativity.

My Rules for leading genius correspond in many ways to how Flexner launched and ran the IAS. These Ten Rules for Leading Genius will give you the special awareness and skill set to lead brilliant people to achieve the breakthroughs that will solve the complex problems you face:

1. Mirrors don't lie.
2. Get out of the way.
3. Shut up and listen.
4. Turn over the rocks.

5. Alchemy outperforms chemistry.
6. Your past is not the future's truth.
7. Ignore squirrels.
8. Harmonize hearts and minds.
9. Let the problem seduce the genius.
10. Make peace with crisis.

RECOGNIZING GENIUS

1

In his early role as an educator, Flexner gained insight into the characteristics that mark a genius. Flexner's father, Moritz, was a hat merchant who lost his business in the financial crisis of 1873. He never recovered from that blow, financially or emotionally and was unable to provide for the education of his children. Flexner's older brother, Jacob, who owned a pharmacy, covered Flexner's tuition at Johns Hopkins University. At Hopkins, Flexner started to think about whether native intelligence needed education to develop into genius.

Though he wanted to continue at Hopkins for graduate school, he was not awarded a scholarship and did not have money for tuition, so he returned to his hometown of Louisville, Kentucky. There, he taught and eventually started a boys' college preparatory school. Just as his older brother helped him financially, Flexner paid for the education of his younger brother, Simon, who became a world-renowned medical pathologist, and for his sister, Mary, to attend Bryn Mawr College.

At his Louisville prep school, Flexner found that threats and compulsion did little to motivate his students. Their intellectual level remained unchanged. He came to believe that if students were free to work as they pleased, they would learn for themselves, because the information mattered to them more than a grade.

Flexner changed how he operated his school—"without rules, without examinations, without records, and without reports."[1] His students began to stay late and come in on weekends for extra study time. When the boys excelled on college entrance exams, he could see that his theory had worked.

Flexner had transformed his students into promising applicants to Ivy League schools. His infectious enthusiasm for education must have had a lot to do with it, but his decision to give his students authority over their education and to focus on learning rather than testing made the critical difference.

He longed to reform education with his ideas, but he stayed in Louisville to help support his family. Flexner would have spent his life feeling trapped there, and the IAS never would have existed, if it were not for his wife, Anne Crawford. While sitting in on a women's writing circle in Louisville, she heard Alice Rice's story of an impoverished widow of good cheer who raises a family amidst remarkable bad luck. Anne turned that book into a play, titled *Mrs. Wiggs and the Cabbage Patch*, which had an extended run on Broadway in 1904, and became a series of movies. Anne made $15,000 in the play's first year, which was a small fortune at the time.

At thirty-nine, Flexner was finally able to launch his plan for reforming college and graduate education nationally. He sold his preparatory school and moved with his wife and their daughter, Jean, to Cambridge, Massachusetts, where he completed a master's degree at Harvard. Then, the family spent two years traveling to various universities in Europe. Wherever they went, Anne's fame as a playwright and her natural charm opened doors for Flexner, which he would never have entered without her. He met many of the foremost writers and thinkers in the United States and Europe through her.

Flexner and his family gravitated to Berlin, the hub of scientific activity for the world at the time. Education at the University of Berlin was of the highest quality. He sat in on lectures by renowned scientists, who inspired him to formulate characteristics of brilliance that stayed with him for the rest of his career. He admired Carl Stumpf, the leading German psychologist, who was able to make the most complex topic clear and exciting. The Nobel Laureate Ernest Rutherford once said, "It should be possible to explain the laws of physics to a barmaid."[2]

Another Berlin professor, the brilliant sociologist Georg Simmel had a restless mind that bounced from topic to topic. Each topic he touched on opened Flexner's eyes to whole new vistas of possibility. Flexner concluded that smart people knew they were in the right position when work became like a game. For Flexner, the common markers of genius included a rigorous but peripatetic mind able to make complexities understandable and to open up new worlds for exploration.

The Making of a Genius

Many social scientists agree with Flexner that until a genius finds the right education and a stimulating environment, brilliance cannot shine. Einstein, who failed high school math and barely got through college, is the iconic example of this phenomenon. Not until late in his twenties, when he began to work in theoretical physics at the University of Bern, did he find something that fascinated him and thus awoke his enormous native intelligence.

Anders Ericsson, a psychologist at Florida State University, proposed the ten-year rule for genius: "Many characteristics once believed to reflect innate talent are actually the result of intense practice extended for a minimum of ten years."[3] Ericsson suggested that focused, deliberate practice over a long period could permit automatic subconscious access to long-term memories, which could generate exceptional creativity.

When I talk with geniuses in my field about their major discoveries, they never tell me how hard it was. Each tells me how much fun the work was. George Scialabba wrote an adage, mistakenly attributed to Albert Einstein, that "Creativity is intelligence having fun."[4] The geniuses I know see their work as fun, which leads me to conclude that an innately brilliant and hard-working person may need one more element before becoming a genius—an inner joy that catalyzes the genius to focus on a single area intensively, 10,000 hours by popular measurement. Whether you define that joy as fun, excitement, or wonder, each genius I have met has that same spark within.

Genius Is Not Like the Rest of Us

We cannot communicate well with genius, because she or he thinks differently from us. When geniuses are solving problems, their intense power of concentration isolates them from others. Their thought processes are fundamentally individualistic and unique. Convincing a genius to think he needs to be part of a team is one of the most challenging aspects of leading someone smarter than you.

Most geniuses master several fields besides their own. Geniuses have extraordinary general intelligence that allows them to understand and enjoy many topics outside their own area of expertise. I have observed geniuses leap nimbly from topic to topic, making connections I could barely follow.

The innate curiosity of brilliant people can make them obsessive. Genius is about immersing oneself in a subject until solutions become obvious. A genius can cut through the fog of complexity to see what no one else does. Geniuses like to see everything fit together. Their ability to color outside the lines and their understanding of how things work in other fields lead to the great leaps they are able to make to solve difficult problems. The other side of the coin is that brilliant people can become distracted by any appealing idea that enters their consciousness.

Most geniuses have hobbies that are passions. Geniuses seek to master a hobby in the same way they master their own fields. Einstein was an expert on Mozart, appreciating the complex, interlocking precision of Mozart's music; Napoleon enjoyed chess; Marie Curie was a long-distance bicyclist, using her rides to review the problems she was dealing with in the lab.

Geniuses perceive the world differently from the rest of us. Extremely intelligent people, who have transcendent insight into unsolvable problems, think on a higher plane than we do. A genius sees things we do not and questions our assumptions. They make new connections and add new meanings to words.

Genius breaks norms and disturbs the status quo. Most of us are uncomfortable with genius, not just because geniuses are often socially awkward, but because they challenge our views and our place in the world. In short, genius upsets the apple cart. Genius dissolves what we think we know and replaces it with a truer vision of reality.

Genius is about living with a subject obsessively, until the problem is penetrated. When geniuses are laser-focused, the problem becomes an imaginary land they are exploring. When working obsessively, it is difficult for geniuses to put themselves in someone else's shoes, to see the world from another point of view. Since communication depends on shared viewpoints, attempting to communicate with a genius can be frustrating.

How a Genius Thinks

Considering historical geniuses reveals several common characteristics of their thought processes, regardless of discipline. Their thoughts zigzag across many fields and ideas, and they approach problems from many angles. Their ideas do not follow predictably from one to another.

Alex Corwin, a physicist from Cornell University, has heard the Nobel Prize-winning physicist Richard Feynman lecture on his major discoveries. He told me that Feynman's best breakthroughs came out of nowhere. They were unpredictable until Feynman explained them, then they seemed simple. Feynman's discoveries were elegant, but they were not obvious. Someone else would not have reached the same revelation. "Feynman saw things no one else did," Corwin said.

When other experts in the field first hear details of an innovation, they often slap their foreheads and say, of course. No one but the genius saw the connections. The finding is obvious only after it is explained. Genius breakthroughs are elegant in their simplicity, but simple does not mean obvious.

"Any intelligent fool can make things bigger and more complex," the economist Ernst Schumacher said. "It takes a touch of genius, and a lot more to move in the opposite direction."[5]

The physicist Murray Gell-Mann once published an equation simply because it was beautiful, even though it went against multiple published experiments. The previous publications turned out to be wrong, and that equation later won him the Nobel Prize.

Einstein often wondered if his equations were beautiful because they were true, or were they true because they were beautiful. He did not want the elegance of the equations to blind him to their accuracy.

When confronted by a problem, most of us think back to what we have learned in the past to find something similar to the current problem. We select related experiences and use those as guides to solve the problem. Educators term this classic thought process "heuristic thinking," which works most of the time, because it is fast and easy, but it produces only incremental gains.

Geniuses, by contrast, think beyond the flashlight of previous experiences. Geniuses are not limited to the pool of light cast by the flashlight. A genius dreams of the world outside the flashlight's illumination.

A group of mathematicians in Göttingen, Germany, invented the four-dimensional geometry that Einstein used to define the relative relationship of space and time. The mathematicians were surprised when Einstein made advances with their invention, which had eluded them. Einstein was able to see new possibilities that had not occurred to them.

Dean Simonton, whose interests as a professor at the University of California Davis include genius, creativity, and leadership, wrote in *Scientific Genius: A Psychology of Science* that all genius starts with the combination of ideas that may seem totally unrelated to the current problem, but can lead to innovative new solutions.[6] The entire work of a genius is a continuous collision and fusion of ideas leading toward discovery.

Geniuses can see hidden relationships, and they often define them visually, rather than by numbers or formulas. The organic chemist F. A. Kekulé dreamed of six snakes in a circle biting each other's tail, and awoke with the structure of benzene in his mind. Nikola Tesla saw a connection between the setting sun's rotation around the Earth and conceived of an alternating current motor, where the magnetic pole rotates inside the engine.

Genius can be immensely productive. Edison held 1,093 patents and set a goal of one invention every ten days. J. S. Bach wrote a cantata every week, and Einstein published more than 248 papers in addition to his groundbreaking work on relativity.

Of course, not every product of genius is world changing. Geniuses can produce massive quantities of creative work that can be worthless. Only a few diamonds can be mined from this huge output. Of Edison's thousand patents, only one is the light bulb.

Recognizing Genius

It is important to understand how a genius thinks so that you can recognize one. Genius is rare and often hidden. There may be a potential genius in your organization who just needs the right spark to reach a transcendent level of intellect. If you can identify a latent genius and provide her with the impetus from further training or a new assignment, you can add immeasurably to the productivity of your team.

Recognizing a genius when you interview one, especially someone young and without a record of accomplishment, is difficult but crucial for your team to go from good to great. One afternoon, I interviewed six biochemists for a position on my research team. My goal was to find the key problem solver for the project, the smartest person among these candidates.

My first impulse when interviewing job candidates is to hire someone like me. In this group of candidates, his name was Jack. Jack had attended Indiana University, where I used to work. I knew his professors, who told me that Jack got to the lab before anyone else and worked like a sled dog. His grades were outstanding.

Jack liked what I liked. He enjoyed running late at night, reading murder mysteries, and watching college football. He had two young girls whom he spoiled despite his wife's admonitions. He laughed easily, especially at my jokes. He solved problems by throwing more hard work at them. When faced with adversity, he redoubled his effort and never quit.

I knew that I would be comfortable with Jack, because he thought the same way I do—logically, incrementally, and reproductively. A genius does not think that way. If I wanted a friend to work with, Jack was the person to hire.

Any team needs people like Jack. The Jacks of the world keep teams together by doing all the small, thankless tasks that no one else wants to do. In fact, Jack could easily be in my position in a decade, leading the team. Jack was like me, which meant he most definitely was not a genius.

I also interviewed a woman named Jill, who immediately rubbed me the wrong way. She did not get my jokes. When I made one, she just stared at me with a perplexed look. My chuckles tailed off awkwardly.

Stuck using the conventional interview questions, I asked, "What was the biggest challenge you faced in your life, and how did you overcome it?"

To answer, she talked about three unrelated life experiences, most of them personal, like getting her car stolen when her laptop was in the trunk. Her interests were not academic, because college and graduate school were boring. Her grades were average, just enough to keep her scholarship.

The only reason I was interviewing her was that she had near-perfect GRE scores, and she had published a paper on statistics even though her graduate program was in biochemistry. Instead of attending one of the major research universities, she went to a small Catholic college.

Though she is Jewish, she chose that school because of its great medieval literature program. She wanted to take electives in that area. She loved both philosophy and virtual computer games.

She had customized her own laptop for role-playing computer games, which was, I realized, why losing her laptop was such a hardship. I have to admit that this tiny insight gave me a feeling of triumph, because the interview was hard work.

She would stop speaking suddenly and leave the conversation hanging in silence. She was not rude or harsh, but her answers to my questions were tangential. She jumped from topic to topic. I kept steering her back to the question I asked, so that I could fill out my evaluation form, but she kept answering a slightly different question, one more interesting to her.

Jill was the anti-me. I knew that working with her would be a challenge. It would be uncomfortable for me, but she was oblivious to the awkwardness between us. She would never have the same social conventions that I do.

I realized that if I wanted someone who could solve the problems that were holding up our team, Jill was a better choice than Jack. Jill thought visually and poetically. She could hold multiple unrelated ideas in her head at once. Connections between medieval poets and computer applications sprung into her head spontaneously.

Jill was highly productive in areas outside her expertise. Whenever she became interested in a new topic, she immersed herself in it until she was an expert. She could lose herself in a problem for hours on end without even realizing she had neglected to eat or sleep.

You have to keep your eyes open to recognize geniuses. You can miss them, because they are not like you, and they can make you uncomfortable. You might miss a genius, because you might not communicate well with one. To recognize a genius, I had to get past the requirement that a person must connect with me and that I must feel comfortable with her or him.

In the end, I hired them both. Jack needs Jill to solve problems, and Jill needs Jack to do the boring stuff that makes the lab function well.

I have learned to ask myself six questions about candidates to assess whether they might be the genius our team needs. These six questions will help you to identify characteristics of the way geniuses think:

1. **Does a candidate think in parallel lines instead of in a single, straight line?** Electricity can run in a linear series or in parallel, in multiple pathways simultaneously. Can a candidate only think about one thing at a time? Alternatively, can he hold more than one concept in his head at the same time, even when the concepts are contradictory? Einstein was able to relate mass to energy when others considered them unrelated. Unless a candidate can hold multiple, seemingly contradictory thoughts in her head at once, she will not be able to see patterns where others see randomness.

2. **Is a potential team member expert in more than one area?** Not only was Leonardo da Vinci one of the most gifted artists in history, he was an inventive visionary. He conceptualized helicopters, tanks, solar power, calculators, and the theory of plate tectonics long before engineering caught up to his ideas. In addition to being a founding father, Ben Franklin was an inventor and scientist whose work influenced physics and electricity. He invented the lightning rod, bifocals, the first public library, and the odometer. In addition to success on the job, does the candidate have hobbies and interests outside his or her field that engage the candidate's creativity? Einstein was a classical violinist and wrote several essays on Mozart.

3. **Does the candidate get lost in the problem he faces?** Does he become obsessed about finding the answers or reaching a goal? Does she approach a challenge with excitement and find joy in the process?

4. **Are the candidate's solutions to problems unexpected yet simple?** Does the candidate view a problem from different points of view? Is he able to think outside the box? Can she communicate complicated thoughts in a simple way?

5. **Is the candidate highly productive?** Edison had an enormous number of patents, and Einstein published hundreds of papers. Of course, not all of those papers were at the same level as his theory of relativity, but his mind continuously produced ideas.

6. **Does the candidate care about being precise in his or her work?** I often cannot recognize whether a genius is precise or not, because I do not understand the work. But I can recognize whether a person cares about being precise. Geniuses have little tolerance for sloppiness in their field, but they can forget the most mundane things, like paying electric bills.

I use these questions to identify a genius in any group of applicants. When you are recruiting new hires or evaluating those already on your team, use these questions to identify outstanding talent. Of course, genius is rare. Finding and recruiting a genius is a coup for any team. If you can discover a genius and manage to integrate her into an effective team, you can make advances that no one would ever have thought possible.

Once you have found and hired your geniuses, you have to know how to work with them effectively. You might think that working with brilliant people would reduce the problems of leadership, not magnify them. After all, a genius can see further and produce breakthroughs more easily. But leading genius requires special strategies.

The following chapter discusses the challenges of leading genius and gives you an understanding of what you need to do to establish cohesive, productive teams.

GENIUS IS NOT ENOUGH

2

You cannot just go to a genius and tell her, "Go invent something and make money." There is no single pathway to discovery, which is why genius has to be led. A leader cannot mandate invention, because discovery is organic and evolves on its own.

Sometimes a breakthrough comes from single-minded persistence. William Shockley worked at Bell Labs for more than ten years with the goal of making the first silicon transistor to replace the bulky vacuum tube. He had the theory down, but could not produce a working model. He called in Walter Brattain and John Bardeen to handle the engineering and development. They worked for two years on the project before succeeding. They built the first transistor, which made the laptop computer and the smartphone possible. Shockley, Bardeen, and Brattain won the Nobel Prize in 1956 for their discovery, which required twelve years of focused work.

In other cases, discoveries occur by chance. Percy Spencer was working at Raytheon on radar for the U.S. Department of Defense. While standing in an active radar field, he noticed the candy bar in his pocket was melting. Spencer could have ignored that melting candy bar, but he immediately realized the implication. From his observation of the melting chocolate, the microwave oven was born.

Leadership can support genius by understanding the best application for a new discovery. Percy Spencer's boss, Laurence Marshall, does not get enough credit for the microwave. Having led Raytheon during World War II, he realized that the end of the war would result in a massive decrease in defense spending, his company's major source of income. The economic environment was changing, and nimble technological advances were needed to keep his company alive. He was desperate to come up with an alternative income stream.

The discussions on the future direction of Raytheon were highly charged. Spencer's idea to use electrical microwaves to heat food was only one of many proposed. The Raytheon engineers all knew their company's survival was at stake. They had been working intensely to invent a technological advance they could bring to market.

Despite great pressure to choose other directions, Marshall picked the microwave oven from numerous concepts using microwaves, such as drying ink or drying tobacco leaves for cigarettes.

Marshall had one chance to get it right, because Raytheon did not have sufficient funds for another attempt. He made the right choice, and that decision not only saved the company but also created a new industry. Spencer's discovery of microwaves has become revered lore in engineering circles, but no one remembers that Marshall made the decision about how to apply the discovery. This story clearly shows that genius alone is not enough for success. Leadership and the broader view it can bring are just as important.

Massive Technological Superiority Is Not Enough

Companies can have an overwhelming technological advantage and still fail. When I was young, "Kodak" was the word for photographs, as we use "Google" to describe Internet searches now. However, Kodak ended up in bankruptcy, because they did not change from film to digital photography fast enough. What killed Kodak is not listening to the innovators in the company who believed that digitization would eventually destroy the film business. Kodak invented digital photography, but film had been making all its money. The inventive geniuses inside Kodak were seen to be threatening Kodak's source of profits. Although Kodak owned many of the patents required for digital photography, it licensed those patents to their competitors.

The CEO at the time was George Fisher, ironically a renowned technological expert. Though midlevel managers reportedly saw the digital revolution coming in the late '80s, complacent senior leaders ignored them, because the company was so profitable. Raytheon's response to innovation was in stark contrast to Kodak's. Raytheon not only recognized the potential of the new technology, but they committed to developing it.

The failure to embrace technological advance is not unique to Kodak. Swiss watchmakers dominated that industry for centuries. They knew how to make bearings, gears, and mainsprings better than anyone. In 1967, the CEH (*Centre Electronique Horloger*, or Center for the Electronic Watch) invented the electronic quartz watch. When Swiss researchers presented the new invention to Swiss manufacturers, every Swiss watchmaking firm rejected it. Blind to the fundamental shift in the world around them, the watchmakers allowed the researchers to display the electronic watch as a novelty at the World Watch Congress that year. Japanese and American companies licensed the new watch and proceeded to create a huge new market.

The leadership of Kodak and the Swiss watchmaking industry did not see their product through the eyes of their consumers, but rather from a business management standpoint. For the consumer, being able to store more than a thousand photos on a palm-sized camera, immediately view and enhance them, and discard the ones they disliked were very appealing. Similarly, consumers wanted a watch that did not need winding and was always accurate. Any manager would find it difficult to abandon a business line with margins like Kodak's. The Swiss had been the world's leading watchmakers for centuries. In 1968, they had 65 percent share of the world watch market. Their success prevented them from seeing that the shift from mechanical to electronic was about to occur. It would have taken daring leadership for these companies to put aside a highly profitable product line with market dominance, but doing so could have grown their companies and saved thousands of jobs.

Why Does Genius Require Special Rules?

What makes leading geniuses complex is their awareness of how smart they are. Though some may view this confidence as arrogance, most often it is a matter of identity. Being brilliant is who they are.

It is difficult to get a genius to abide by rules. They got to where they are by ignoring convention and transcending logic in their thinking. They see no problem in behaving in a way that conflicts with the culture of the team. They ignore company processes, preferring to solve problems their own way. Extremely smart employees think that they know more than you about the team's task. They focus on what they need to complete the job, not on you as a leader. This turns the tables on leadership. Though most people in an organization look up to their leaders, geniuses focus more on the value they bring to the equation themselves.

In short, geniuses do not like to be led. They know their worth to the company, and they know it's likely higher than yours. For the most part, geniuses do not care about titles or promotions, because their motives are complex and individual. They are often connected to a network of like-minded friends throughout the world, who are just a click away. Dissembling fools none of them, and they have no tolerance for excuses.

Deep down inside, a genius may easily be his own most strident critic, much harsher than you would ever be in your judgments. That does not mean you can routinely criticize the performance of geniuses. Your critique lacks legitimacy in their eyes, because you are not as smart as they are. The genius may see your job as an insignificant contribution, and never thank you for anything you have done. As you can see, leading genius poses particular challenges.

From my experience leading large groups of smart people, I learned that many of them think they could do my job better than I. And they could, if the job was only about their project or their specialized area of expertise. But being a leader is so much more than that. It's about seeing how all the dots connect and come together to make a complex yet integrated product. Though a leader must maintain a view of the organization as a whole and make judgments based on the whole, employees are often directed toward small dots. When leading a team of regular employees, a directive approach can work to coordinate the individual parts of the whole. That will not work with geniuses. Brilliant, creative employees often have excellent reasons for actions that benefit their project, but which might be detrimental to the whole company. A leader has to articulate how a decision will affect the whole team. If the leader has generated a strong team culture, a genius will accept decisions that he or she understands, which will help the good of the entire team.

Geniuses are not motivated by the same things as most employees. Usually, the challenge is to motivate people to do tasks that they find mundane or dislike. In technical fields dominated by the super-intelligent, the challenge is to motivate geniuses to work toward the good of the company as a whole, rather than just advance their careers or their interests. A genius needs to be motivated to take others into consideration and think of the success of the team as his own success.

Building an Environment Conducive to Creativity

Most of the brilliant scientists I have led did not think they needed me. In fact, I got the feeling that my leadership bored them. I was too slow, too needy, and too obvious for them. Getting geniuses to accept that they need a non-genius to be successful is one of the challenges of leading genius. For me, boring was beautiful, because I had succeeded in providing an environment in which geniuses could focus on their work.

Brilliant engineers, scientists, and creative people have a unique set of needs. To lead geniuses, you have to reject traditional notions of leadership. You have to be more of an unseen manager who provides data, support, and process without dictating solutions or directions.

You can provide the problem, all the known data, and the resources, but you cannot tell geniuses how to solve the problem. If you do, you undercut their intrinsic capability to be creative, to generate a groundbreaking solution. You have to lead without being too direct, which is much harder than it sounds. You are the best leader when you guide geniuses to discover the right decision for themselves, not when you dictate what that decision should be. Leading geniuses requires you to lead by providing choices, not directions.

Although telling a genius what to do is much easier than allowing individual autonomy, such a directed approach can establish boundaries that limit finding creative solutions to complex problems. On the other hand, you can also become too passive and let a genius figure out the goals on her own. Your job is to support problem solving and to keep the geniuses focused on the goal. The balance between freeing and focusing creativity is one of the most difficult tasks of leading geniuses. Some distractions, like Spencer and microwaves, are worthy of pursuing, but others are a waste of everyone's time. A leader needs to decide if a distraction is more valuable than the original problem. To manage geniuses, you have to become a leader in an untraditional sense: You support a process without defining the means and sometimes even the ends.

Instead of assuming that what you do has the greatest influence on the success of a project, you have to understand that a leader of geniuses shapes the environment in which success is achieved. What you control is only indirectly related to the project's specific goals and success. A leader of geniuses does not cause the chemical reaction. You are the crucible that holds the reaction.

You can change research infrastructure, the team size, and the focus of the team, but team success comes from the creativity of its members. The environment in which a genius works fosters her or his creativity, which ultimately has an important effect on the outcome. Anyone can get lucky once, but if you see a leader whose teams make advance after advance over the long haul, that is a sure sign that the leader knows how to work with geniuses.

Genius Does Not Lead Genius Well

If you are feeling insecure about your ability to lead geniuses, remember that really smart people can make poor leaders. Although there are notable exceptions, such as Gates and Musk, brilliant people usually do not lead other brilliant people well, because they always give more weight to their own intelligence than to any other consideration, even data. Geniuses tend to discount anything they do not know, which constricts their decision-making ability. A non-genius can more easily see outside the problem to the needs of the entire organization.

The more deeply geniuses explore a problem, really getting down inside it, immersing themselves, the harder it is for them to see outside the problem. Someone who is not a genius has more balance and can have a broader perspective on the project. As a leader, you might not see the solution, but you recognize what solving the problem means for everyone. The reason you can lead geniuses is because you are not a genius.

When geniuses lead a project, they tend to tell everyone what to do. Certain they know more than anyone else, they cannot resist dictating the best path forward. They think the project will fail unless they define every task and believe all their assessments are correct.

William Shockley, the genius who led the Bell Lab team that developed the silicon transistor, had difficulty leading other brilliant scientists and engineers. After he won the Nobel Prize in 1956 with John Bardeen and Walter Brattain, he founded Shockley Semiconductor and hired sixty of the smartest people in the world. Then he proceeded to disenfranchise his own geniuses.

Shockley was dictatorial and did not give reasons for his decisions. He ignored employees' reports, which he had assigned himself. He once gave a research paper he wrote to some of his junior scientists and told them to submit the paper for publication under their names, implying they would never be able to do the same quality of investigation.

Eight of his best employees, including Bob Noyce and Gordon Moore, soon left to form Fairchild Semiconductor in 1957.

The eight engineers who defected from Shockley Semiconductor went on to found many of the most famous computer companies in history, including Intel, Advanced Micro Devices, and National Semiconductor. Had Shockley not been so condescending and arrogant, the defections may never have happened, and Shockley Semiconductor would have made the chip inside the laptop on which I typed these words, not Intel.

When a genius leads geniuses, his decision making can be self-centered. Leaders must maintain a view of the organization as a whole and make judgments based upon that whole. Geniuses often cannot step back to see the whole picture, because their immense power of concentration keeps them focused on a single problem, which can lead them to favor their project over others.

A genius may have intelligent and creative reasons why her project should be favored, but if these reasons were applied to every project equally, a different strategic decision might result. By not applying her reasoning equitably, a genius can play favorites without knowing it.

A genius may not evaluate his own work very well. Rather than admit failure early in a project to permit resource redirection, a genius may see the problem he faces as inordinately significant, because he is the person thinking about it. He may continue to pour time and funding into the problem beyond its value. Geniuses may give more weight to what interests them than is deserved in the marketplace of ideas. The issue with this approach is that a genius does not decide what is a commercial success, the public does, and we the public are not that smart.

Managing Egos

One of the most sensitive areas to navigate in leading geniuses is managing their egos. They can be self-involved and overconfident. Exceptionally smart people often misjudge their proficiency in unrelated areas. A leader must manage this tendency without alienating the genius. You have to strike a balance between engendering confidence and discouraging reckless self-importance. There is a difference between believing you will succeed at a task and having an inflated sense of self.

Most business leaders gather data, make a decision, and impose it. "I am the decider," George Bush famously said, and countless CEOs have echoed the attitude since.[1] Such a mindset is risky when leading geniuses, because imposing a decision on geniuses without their buy-in is ego-bruising. If decisions are made for them, they will intellectually withdraw from the project. The best way to get a genius to alter his path is to let him discover the rationale for change himself, rather than having it imposed on him. Providing data and letting a genius derive his own conclusions is a good mechanism for managing egos during a decision-making process.

Another way to control the egos of geniuses is to surround them with brilliant people, who serve as a reality check for self-importance. Relationships with other very smart people can help to keep the ego of a genius in check.

One leader in the aerospace engineering industry confided to me that when his team began feeling a little too good about themselves and started becoming complacent, he brought in a few world-renowned engineers to review their work. "Those guys spotted flaws in the work really fast. If your work was not up to par, you were in trouble," he said. As mentioned, Flexner brought visiting scientists to the IAS to stimulate novel ideas and keep the faculty grounded.

Team Cohesion Versus Individual Creativity

Another challenge of leading brilliant people involves balancing creativity and team cohesion. Cohesion during the course of a project is essential to reaching the goal. There is little room for diversions generated by a genius. When you lead geniuses, you must strike a balance between directing individuals toward team goals and encouraging innovation that could lead to a breakthrough. Valuing cohesion over innovation, leaders often employ a top-down strategy. The leader assigns each individual a task. This does not work well for teams that include a genius, because the genius will be dissatisfied with an assignment, and creativity will take a nose dive.

Both cohesion and innovation are important. A leader cannot value one over the other. At Shockley Semiconductor, Shockley made innovation more important than cohesion. He once developed a secret project within the company, with only a select few working on it. Those assigned to the special project felt exceptional, an exclusive club of experts. The secret project members had more resources and were allowed to be more creative. Those not included in the secret project sensed that they were left out and lost the motivation to complete the original project. Shockley created a group with special privileges, which destroyed the cohesion of the original team. Many left the company as a result.

Balancing Between the Pilot and the Passenger

A leader of geniuses cannot simply be the pilot, dictating every decision. At the same time, a leader cannot be only a passenger, allowing the genius to travel wherever she will. The challenge of being Einstein's boss is to maintain this delicate balance.

Leading Einstein is like having one foot on each side of a balance scale on top of a pyramid. On one side of the pyramid is the tendency to let your team have complete freedom to make all the decisions affecting the direction of the project. In this case, they carry you as if you were a passenger on a plane.

On the other side of the pyramid, you make all the decisions about direction and resources. You are the pilot. In that situation, you will suppress the individual creativity of your genius. She or he will become passive and lose initiative, as shown in Figure 2.1.

Pilots value team equity, purpose, and cohesion above creative distractions and individual innovation. On the other hand, if you as the leader become a passenger along for the ride, you risk permitting distractions and then will fail to meet organizational goals. Overemphasizing either aspect of leading geniuses will lead to diminished productivity.

Finding balance between the two extremes of leadership is the only way to achieve top performance by a genius. Maintaining this balance does not mean you avoid putting weight on either side of the scale. You have to stand equally on both sides. The best leader of geniuses actively uses team cohesion and individual innovation simultaneously. Having one foot weighted equally on each pan of the scale is the only way to achieve maximal productivity. Using both sides equally, the balanced leader is flexible. A good leader is both pilot and passenger, working to achieve shared goals while promoting individual creativity at the same time.

If you are wondering how you are going to manage this balancing act, my Ten Rules for Leading Genius will be your blueprint for creating an environment that supports innovation, productivity, and success, an environment that allows geniuses to flourish on a united team.

Introduction to the Rules

Some of my Rules may seem like common sense to you, but as we will discuss, it is the simplest mistakes that destroy organizations. Not all of them are specific to genius. After all, very few people are consistently brilliant, world-changing geniuses. These strategies also apply to leading people who are just smarter or more highly specialized than you. The Rules can benefit people who have one shining moment of insight, which results in a great advance. As a leader, relying on those who have proven their genius in the past is obvious. However, sometimes a person can have a flash of brilliance because he is in the right place at the right time. Being a great leader of genius includes spotting that flash and seizing the moment when an ordinary person has a brilliant insight.

Making these guidelines a habit is essential, because they will shape the personality of your team. If these Rules become habitual, you can maintain the productivity and focus of teams of geniuses over an extended period, even in the face of crisis.

It can be difficult to follow the Rules in critical situations, which is when they are needed most. As the complexity and stress of a situation rise, staying on track gets harder. In the past, I have failed to follow my own Rules. I have learned that each Rule builds on the others. Failure in one can lead to a domino effect. When I have broken my own Rules, the harmonious atmosphere I worked to achieve fell apart. The disruption undercut our progress toward our goals. Fortunately, the Rules can resolve the crises I have caused. Even when I make mistakes, simply returning to these guidelines helps to get things running smoothly again.

The following overview is an introduction to the Rules for working productively with geniuses, the core purpose of this book. Each of the succeeding chapters focuses on one of the Rules. In addition to explaining how to implement the Rules, we discuss the barriers that might inhibit you from applying them, and then provide ways to get around those barriers.

The Ten Rules for Leading Genius

1.
MIRRORS DON'T LIE

The first Rule of leading genius is to recognize that you are not a genius, and the genius working for you knows it. This can be painful. It might feel better to lie to yourself about who you are. If you are like most of us, you defend your self-esteem at all costs. Also, it is difficult to assess yourself effectively without a mirror, an impartial advisor you trust to reflect your true self back to you.

To lead geniuses successfully, you have to be ruthless in your self-assessment. If you deceive yourself, you become frozen at that point in your development as a leader. If you cannot evaluate your leadership accurately and make corrections when necessary, you will be ineffective, and you will drag your team down with you. Good leaders can realistically assess how they are doing, but great leaders can correct their behavior based on what they find.

2.
GET OUT OF THE WAY

The single biggest impediment to the success of a genius is you, the leader. If you get in the way of the train of thought of geniuses, they will smash into you, and you could derail them. Stay out of their way. Most leaders think they need to be central to a project in order to direct it. Being too involved limits the creativity of geniuses and slows the problem-solving process. You can only get out of the way if you understand your place in the creative process, which rigorous self-assessment should reveal.

3.
SHUT UP AND LISTEN

Leaders of geniuses tend to talk too much and listen too little. Having a brilliant, captive audience is personally gratifying, but the more you talk, the less you can lead. One of the best methods you can use to get out of the way of a genius is to listen more effectively. When you shut up and listen, you allow genius to be the creative engine of your team, which enhances the team's productivity. Creative listening, which I explain in detail later (see Chapter 5), is the best method for enhancing communication with geniuses and promotes their ownership of the project. Listening to what they say validates the intelligence of geniuses and builds their connection with the team.

4.
TURN OVER THE ROCKS

We all have ways to hide our personal agendas, which are like pale, squirmy bugs found under garden rocks. Our unspoken agenda often benefits us more than the team. The only way to be perceived as authentic is to turn over the rocks for your team to see all the bugs. This means that there is no difference between what you think and what you do, even when it is embarrassing. What may be sufficient transparency for a standard employee is often not enough for a genius. A genius will immediately figure out if you are not being genuine, even if you feel you are not hiding anything. When that happens, a genius will lose trust in you and stop listening.

A good leader of genius provides the rationale for all decisions. A great leader does this before finalizing a decision and welcomes feedback to alter the decision. You should provide the data and interpretation behind any decision before anyone even asks. If a genius has to ask, it is too late.

5.
ALCHEMY OUTPERFORMS CHEMISTRY

Science and technology are now a team sport, more like football than golf. The problems are big enough that they require teams of multiple geniuses. Each genius works on a sliver of a problem. Each has a crucial position to play. A team composed of complementary expertise with a brilliant person assigned to each needed role is predictable chemistry. The output is expected to equal the input. This approach is not enough to create a highly productive team. The best teams of genius are nonlinear with flattened hierarchies that facilitate many unpredictable interactions.

The personalities of team members are just as important as their expertise and intellect. Like alchemy, mixing individual personalities together to form a nonlinear team requires an understanding of the psychology of genius as well as a grasp of each individual's talents. The goal is to create a reaction among the team in which the output is greater than the input, like turning lead into gold.

Leading through chemistry finds the holes in the team's expertise and plugs brilliant people in to fill them. The alchemist looks beyond the obvious needs for expertise to create a nonlinear team in which random collisions generate enormous creativity.

6.
YOUR PAST IS NOT THE FUTURE'S TRUTH

If you are like most of us, no matter how you describe the way you make decisions, you trust your own instincts and experience more than you trust data. That is one way you lie to yourself. You are unconsciously anchored to your last good or bad experience, because your emotions give certain memories more weight. This is especially true of situations in which you have lost a valued team member or a resource. Your brain is wired for loss aversion.

Unless you are intentional about your decisions, you will be biased against reasonable risk, without which there is no creative gain. A good leader uses data to make decisions. A great leader uses the right data, analyzed in an unbiased manner, and applies it to the decision process. A genius will immediately recognize when your decision is based on your own unfounded bias or a past experience and will not take your decision seriously.

7.
IGNORE SQUIRRELS

Many geniuses are like Labrador retrievers, who can be focused on the bone they are chewing, but cannot stop themselves from chasing a squirrel that darts by. A good idea can flash in the mind of a genius, and boom, they are off chasing it. Most leaders try to stay laser focused on the core mission. Geniuses can drive such leaders crazy, because brilliant minds are always pursuing squirrels, those small but interesting ideas outside the core assignment that grab their attention. Novel ideas come in abundance to a genius. Though most of these flashes are irrelevant or not feasible, some distractions turn out to be worth billions. A great leader will wisely choose which squirrels to chase, because a genius cannot chase everything. A leader can add value to a team of genius by having the wisdom to recognize a worthwhile distraction.

8.
HARMONIZE HEARTS AND MINDS

A genius is often regarded to be like a computer, uncaring and unfeeling. We think we can feed data in and out comes the desired product. On the contrary, most geniuses can only achieve what their hearts let them. They are caught and driven by the same emotions as the rest of us. Their hearts can still rule their minds.

Sometimes a genius's heart does not keep up with his head. He might have impressive intellectual gifts, but his emotions can limit those gifts. He may show up for work, but his heart is not in the job. To be productive at the level needed to make significant leaps, the heart of a genius has to be engaged. A genius has to care deeply and emotionally about a problem. For a genius to work at full capacity, he must feel cared for and safe in a warm and supportive environment. Geniuses need to feel they matter to you and to the team, not only for what they do, but also for who they are.

Only when the brain and the heart of a genius are synchronized can a complex problem be fully attacked. The complex emotions of geniuses can limit their innovation, because when stressed they cannot let their minds roam free. The heart must release the brain of a genius to create.

9.
LET THE PROBLEM SEDUCE THE GENIUS

It's rarely effective to push geniuses to change direction. Their problem-solving focus is so intense that it can be difficult to get them to head where you want them to go. Geniuses will resist altering their course if they know you are pushing. Flogging them until they change goals rarely works. They can resist far longer than you can push.

A good leader is able to nudge geniuses toward an important goal, but a great leader can make geniuses own a goal as their own. The most effective leader frames the problem in a way that entices a genius, captures the mind of a genius, and inexorably draws her toward the goal. Geniuses will be far more motivated to solve a problem if they become enamored with the problem on their own.

10.
MAKE PEACE WITH CRISIS

Crisis is the new normal when you are leading brilliant people. Genius by definition is disruptive. Get used to it, because the crises will never stop coming. You must understand and accept that your life will be one crisis after another.

To lead a team of geniuses, you must first lead yourself. If you melt down with every crisis, you will distract the geniuses with the crisis. Losing their focus on the project, they will become less creative. Radiating an inner centeredness demonstrates that the weight of your values is greater than the force of the storm around you. Your stability can keep your geniuses focused on the project. A good leader of geniuses remains calm in the face of crisis, while a great leader also identifies and neutralizes what caused the crisis.

RULE 1:
MIRRORS DON'T LIE

3

Deep inside, we all think we are geniuses. To lead genius, you must recognize that you are not a genius, and the genius working for you knows it. It is painful to see yourself as less intelligent than another, so you lie to yourself to feel better. If you think you don't do this, you are probably deceiving yourself.

Lying to yourself about who you really are produces a fundamental change in how you lead. You become frozen in place. You will avoid making any decision that alters your self-image, which will stifle creativity and prevent innovative advances. Only through rigorous self-reflection can you hope to avoid deceiving yourself.

Early in his tenure at the IAS, Flexner was able to take criticism and reflect on its merits. At the start, he sought opinions from multiple geniuses, including future Supreme Court Justice Felix Frankfurter. Frankfurter questioned launching the Institute with a mathematics department, because he believed it would not lead to any practical advances.

Rather than shying away from this criticism, Flexner embraced it. Although Flexner ultimately held his ground and made the right decision to begin the IAS with a mathematics department, Frankfurter's barrage of criticism served to sharpen Flexner's ideas and ensure they were sound.

Frankfurter joined the board of the IAS and became an important sounding board for Flexner. Later in Flexner's time at the IAS, he did not have the money to equalize salaries. When Frankfurter criticized the inequity, Flexner forced him off the IAS board. If Flexner had evaluated the situation more accurately, he would have owned the salary inequity and worked to rectify it. Instead, he spent a good deal of political capital to force Frankfurter out, a disruption of major proportions.

Being ruthlessly honest about yourself may sound simplistic as Rule 1 for leading genius, but your foundation for growth and improvement needs to be your authentic self, and that is likely not a genius. The practice of self-assessment should be planned like an athlete's workout. Abraham Flexner needed this book, not Albert Einstein.

Einstein and the Bomb

Perhaps the most famous self-evaluation and correction ever to occur in science was Einstein's ultimate opposition to nuclear weapons. In 1939, his friend, the Hungarian physicist Leo Szilard, became aware that the Germans had stopped selling uranium from the Czech mines under their control. This action could only mean that the Germans knew that uranium could be the source of a nuclear chain reaction that could be weaponized.

Einstein promoted the U.S. efforts to develop a nuclear weapon by sending President Roosevelt a letter warning of the German efforts to build an atomic bomb. Szilard wrote the letter detailing the potential for a German nuclear weapon. Szilard did not want the letter to get filed away by a bureaucrat in the State Department, so he imposed on his friend, Alexander Sachs, an economist and advisor to Roosevelt, to hand deliver the letter.

After reading the letter, which Einstein signed, Roosevelt convened a group of scientific and military leaders to investigate whether a nuclear weapon was possible. This led to the Manhattan Project in Los Alamos, New Mexico, which resulted in the first nuclear weapon.

The scientists at Los Alamos had to discover how to separate the uranium that could be used for a nuclear explosion from bulk uranium. One of the project's leaders, Vannevar Bush, visited Einstein in secret to ask his advice without telling him too much about the classified project. At that meeting, Einstein likely provided advice on the method finally used to enrich the reactive uranium.

After the first and second atomic bombs were dropped on Japan, Einstein was appalled at the slaughter of civilians. He deeply regretted sending the letter to Roosevelt, because Germany was defeated by the time the atomic bomb was ready to use. He publicly opposed the development of the more powerful hydrogen bomb.

Einstein suggested that an international committee of scientists should be given control of all nuclear technology to ensure that it was used only for peaceful purposes, such as generating electricity. He devoted much of his last few years to promoting peace and nuclear disarmament.

Looking back, he later said that he had not thought nuclear weapons were possible and that he himself played no role in their development, except for signing a letter to the president. Even Einstein was not truthful to himself. He chose to overlook the power of his recommendation and his constant communication with Szilard on his work separating weapons-grade uranium. His later assessment of his involvement was not consistent with what actually happened.

Success Makes Self-Assessment Harder

It is easier to assess your performance after failure than after success. Even Einstein lied to himself as he corrected his course of action. Success makes us think we are better than we are. It blinds us to our weaknesses and propels us to take risks, which we would not have taken ordinarily.

Long-Term Capital Management is an example of how success can make self-evaluation more difficult. John Meriwether, a former vice chairman at Salomon Brothers, founded Long-Term Capital Management in 1994. It was enormously successful for the first few years but ended up collapsing in a spectacular fashion. By 2000, creditors had gutted it of assets, and the corporation terminated.

The reason for this debacle involves a sophisticated computer program to predict markets, which had been written by the fund managers. They were proud of their efforts to build this program, and they touted its complexity to investors. The sophistication of this program gave them a greater sense of security than was warranted. Their computer algorithm failed to anticipate basic economic issues that were obvious even to the casual market observer. Despite the errors, the managers at Long-Term Capital Management kept raising their investments when they should have been lowering them.

Long-Term Capital Management institutionalized hubris by programming it into their computer algorithm, and this led to massive failures. The beginning of organizational failure is often overconfidence derived from success. Teams become arrogant and begin to regard success as an entitlement. They lose sight of what created that success in the first place.

Warning Signs of Hubris

The uncanny ability of humans to deceive themselves is frightening. I can see it in myself. I believe in my own invincible judgment, and it can become a self-reinforcing logic: If I bet on it, it must win, because I bet on it. Since I am always right, whatever I bet on will win. If you see any of the signs that follow, it's time for ruthless self-assessment:

- **A feeling of entitlement.** This can be quite subtle. For example, you might feel you deserve to be in charge, because you have the most innate talent. If we think we deserve our position because of our own intrinsic value rather than how we perform, we are feeling entitled.

  Entitlement can progress to the point that you feel you deserve to be the leader simply because of who you are. Entitlement can lead to risky choices for which you do not feel accountable. Shirking accountability is a key sign of a sense of entitlement.

■ **You prefer your own opinions to the opinions and ideas of others.** Not only do you attach more value to your opinions, but you also invest part of your own self-worth in the opinions you hold. When one of your opinions is criticized, you become defensive, as if you are being personally attacked. It becomes difficult to judge your own ideas and those of others in an unbiased way. Hubris leads to close-mindedness, which makes you stop learning anything new.

■ **You start emphasizing accountability over creative problem solving.** The message becomes, "I am not to blame, but I sure as hell will find out who is!" This attitude can lead the team to finger-pointing. Improving process takes a back seat to politics. Promotions go to anyone who is adept at escaping blame, instead of to someone who accepts responsibility.

Habitual self-assessment means recognizing mistakes fast, owning them, and acknowledging them publicly. Then you must change, because a genius is naturally skeptical. The manager who says, "I am sorry, that was a mistake," and follows with a "but" and a rationalization is on her way to losing her team.

Only a humble leader can make an apology or give a compliment without a "but." Any added rationale after an apology or a compliment only detracts from its value. How you accept blame or give credit is just as important as whether you do it or not.

True leaders own their errors and create a culture of responsibility. This culture will spill over into every area of the project. If a leader is accountable for her or his actions, then team members will own their niche in a project, and everyone will become more productive.

Faking Humility

Many years ago, a scientist gave me a gift for helping him spin off a company from the university. I waved it away, saying: "It was nothing. I was just doing my job."

Driving home that night, I realized I had just dismissed an event that was important in the life of that scientist. I acted as if the life's dream for this genius was nothing, and I had ruined the significance of the occasion for him. I was being falsely humble, but I did more than that, I denigrated another's achievement, one that meant a lot to him.

That night at home, I emailed him a note telling him how much that compliment meant to me and how much he meant to me as a colleague. I wrote that his appreciation was the best reward I could ever obtain from my work. That scientist has remained a close friend, even as our jobs have taken us farther apart.

Self-assessment starts when a leader accepts himself as limited and prone to mistakes, and recognizes that he makes essential contributions by correcting his mistakes. There is a peace in this balance between forgiving yourself for making a mistake and working harder to make sure it never happens again. If you forgive yourself but never correct yourself in the future, you will lose credibility.

Self-loathing is related to this form of false humility. For years, whenever I made a mistake, I would internally flagellate myself, calling myself an idiot. This anger at myself implied I was shocked that I made the error. I acted as if I should be perfect, like God. This subconscious expectation that I should be perfect was an enormous self-deception.

Self-pity is a consequence of false humility as well. Self-pity comes when you feel that you do not deserve to be wrong. This is unfair, you think. You cannot wallow in self-pity, forgive yourself too easily, and bemoan the consequences as unfair when you make a mistake. No one will join you there.

Laughter as an Antidote for Hubris

Hubris begins with taking ourselves too seriously. Laughter frees us from the artificial constructs we use to feel better about our weaknesses. Laughing at myself shows I own my foibles, they do not own me. They do not control what I believe or how I behave. If I can laugh at myself, I know that I can keep hubris in check.

During the nonviolent uprising in Egypt against President Hosni Mubarak in the Arab Spring of 2011, young intellectuals leading the uprising used Twitter to mock Mubarak. They said that laughing at Mubarak made him less of a threat. It deposed him in their heads. In the same way, laughing at yourself takes you off the throne in your head. When you can see humor in what you do, it's hard to think of yourself as infallible. Laughing is a physiological release from the constraints that hold you in a certain mindset.

You can systematically incorporate humor into your leadership as a means of maintaining your humility. I email a funny story once a month to the entire department. I use myself as an example in a humorous or embarrassing situation as often as possible. I once gave a bottle of expensive Scotch as a gift to an Islamic friend. It took him a year before he told me that his religion forbade him from drinking it. I was mortified and apologized profusely. My awkward embarrassment and apology made him laugh heartily and created a bond between us that lasts to this day.

Early in his career, Einstein took himself very seriously, but as he grew older and the accolades came, he learned to laugh at himself. Near the end of his life, Princeton held an all-day series of lectures in his honor. Einstein sat through the lectures without any complaints or comments. Someone asked if the lectures had been tiring for him. "They would have been tiring if I had understood them!" Einstein responded.[1]

As his health deteriorated, his doctor gave him a strict diet, which precluded candy and tobacco. After one dinner at his house, a box of candy was passed around. He held the box for a moment and took a deep sniff. His guests looked at him quizzically. "That's all my doctor allows me to do," he said. "The devil has put a penalty on all the things we enjoy in life."[2]

Gift-Giving and Gratitude

Gift-giving is another antidote to hubris. Formally recognizing the accomplishment of a team member by making a gift takes the spotlight off you and puts it on someone else. The gift should not be too large or expensive to avoid bringing the attention back to you. Planning the gift is as important as giving it. It takes your mind off yourself and focuses it on someone else.

The way you give a gift can make the event a team celebration or a flop. When you give the gift, you call attention to the recipient. You should keep your comments short and let the recipient speak about what the team is celebrating.

You should plan gift-giving events often. The gifts should come from your sense of gratitude for how that person helped the team, or it will seem fake. Gratitude fights a sense of entitlement. When you expect extraordinary effort from your team as your due without recognizing or rewarding them, you imply that you deserve their effort by virtue of your position. This entitlement demeans and devalues your team members, which will greatly diminish their engagement and loyalty.

When you take joy in someone's excitement at receiving an unexpected gift, without thinking of what you will gain from the event, you earn a brief moment of humility. The moment will be brief, because all of us return to thinking about ourselves.

Overcoming Fear of Conflict

True self-assessment means that you must be able to stomach internal conflict. There will always be conflict between how you should be and how you are. Unless you face that friction, you will lie to yourself that things are fine and thus you will never improve. You will never be able to take the justified criticism of colleagues and use their observations to improve.

The IAS originally had consistent funding from the Louis Bamberger and Mrs. Felix Fuld Foundation. Bamberger brother and sister, Louis and Caroline (Mrs. Fuld), along with two partners, built a department store chain in New Jersey and sold it to Macy's shortly before the stock market crash of 1929.

Flexner found that the Bambergers hated conflict at board meetings, even when it was about an important issue. To avoid making the Bambergers uncomfortable with heated discussions, IAS board meetings were ritualistic and monotonous. Nothing was submitted to the board without prior approval by Louis Bamberger. Most board meetings consisted of one member after another reading items into the minutes, without open discussion of issues.

When Harvard lawyer Felix Frankfurter argued passionately against setting widely disparate salaries for faculty members during a board meeting, Louis's sister, Caroline Fuld, leaned over to Flexner and whispered that Frankfurter had to go. Flexner was only too happy to oblige her, as by this time, he had tired of Frankfurter's constant criticisms about how he was running the IAS. Flexner had lost the ability to live with the inherent conflict in self-assessment.

Only Flexner could convince the Bamberger family to make difficult decisions, and so the IAS board became dependent on Flexner alone. The reluctance to face conflict led to a lack of self-assessment not only by the Bambergers, but also by Flexner. More than any one reason, this is why Flexner lost the backing of the IAS faculty, which contributed to his downfall.

The Third Way

A leader of genius must be able to consider two conflicting concepts equally and simultaneously. The leader then has to resolve the tension between the ideas by generating a new approach that contains elements of each but is better than either alone. This process is called "integrative self-reflection." Integrative self-reflection requires you to be comfortable with a situation that usually provokes anxiety: holding two opposing views of yourself in your head at the same time.

Integrative self-reflection does not imply that one virtue is more important than another. You do not have to categorize your behavior and decisions as good or bad. There is often a Third Way of resolving your personal leadership flaws as well as resolving team conflicts.

If you make a costly mistake, you need your intellect to recognize and learn from it. You need your emotions to cement any lessons learned. You must balance your emotions and intellect without discarding either. You can calmly accept that you are flawed and set your mind like flint toward avoiding the same mistakes in the future.

The Third Way is a creative path forward that takes into account both poles of a conflict without invalidating either. The Third Way recognizes that the two poles may never be completely reconciled, but that both are useful in different situations. Both poles have value that you should retain, because they balance each other.

Integrative self-reflection can discover that the underlying motivations of the two poles may overlap, which will help define a Third Way. The Third Way is not obvious and can be hard to arrive at, but it can point you toward personal growth as a leader. The Third Way makes leadership an art.

Einstein provided a great example of a Third Way when confronted with conscientious objectors to military service during World War II. He wrote to the King of Belgium suggesting that such conscientious objectors could still be drafted into service by being assigned to critical but nonmilitary support services, like merchant ships or hospital wards. Many Western nations adopted this approach, fulfilling both the pacifists' ideals and national needs.

Methods of Integrative Self-Reflection

Peter Drucker, an organizational expert, proposed a method for holding yourself accountable. He advised that you record what you expect to happen whenever you make a decision or take an important action. Nine or twelve months later, compare the real-world results of your decisions with what you had expected. Consider whether you were right or wrong, and then apply what you have learned about your assumptions to your next decision. This method appeals to me as a scientist. We test whether our hypothesis is correct, and then we analyze the data and adjust the next decision based on that data.

Another technique for self-assessment is to list the specific values that guide a decision. The goal of this exercise is to identify the values upon which you act, not those you think you hold. If the values guiding your decisions do not match those you or the organization holds, that identifies areas you need to address.

Recognition Is Not the Same as Correction

Being ruthless in self-assessment is not enough. You actually have to correct the errors and weaknesses you identify. This means being flexible and patient, because it takes time and practice. The practice of self-assessment must be planned in detail, like the athlete's workout mentioned above.

You have to learn to engineer self-disruption. This is more like sculpting marble than molding clay. Our internal constructs are more fixed in stone than we think. We fear the noise and mess of self-correction. We think we are more productive when the road is smooth, but that is not true. Huge technological advance takes place under disruptive stress.

You have to identify thoughts about yourself that are universal, true no matter what. Examples of such thoughts range from "I always make the team feel good about themselves" to the opposite, "I never can get the team to see the big picture." Always and never are totalizing statements, which are obviously not true. There are probabilities and there are possibilities, but our character and our decisions are neither forever or never. "I think it's much more interesting to live not knowing than to have answers which might be wrong. I have approximate answers and possible beliefs and different degrees of uncertainty about different things," the physicist Richard Feynman said.[3]

It is more comforting to bracket your life in totalizing statements, instead of having to weigh each situation independently. If you define yourself in terms of totalizing statements, you lose the possibility of personal growth. You will not see anything outside the brackets.

The question is how do you free your true self from the rigid captivity that is your idea of yourself? This is where traditional business paradigms break down. The goal of self-assessment in most organizations is to improve your outcomes. The goal of self-assessment in leading genius is to enhance the discoveries of the genius. It is not about you, but about enhancing the potential of geniuses for discovery.

Consider the diagram shown in Figure 3.1. The circle on the right represents what your team needs from you and the twisted hexagon represents what you are. The goal of self-reflection is to improve your fit with the team. The figure at the left of this illustration represents a poor fit with the team, because the leader cannot evaluate himself.

Self-reflection is the ability to look inward at yourself objectively. It is the first step in assessing your strengths and weaknesses of character. If you are unable to correct your flaws, you are doomed to repeat all your mistakes, and you will never understand why things went wrong. You will prevent your team from reaching its potential. The first steps to self-assessment will shift your focus from your own success, but in themselves do not automatically lead to self-correction. You have to work at that.

Self-Assessment Exercise with a Mirror

No matter how much we want to, we cannot change ourselves, because we do not see ourselves as we really are. We need a mirror external to ourselves.

Select a trusted external advisor to serve as that mirror. This person should not be on your team and should have enough distance from you that he will not hesitate to say difficult things. The toughest part of this process is to get yourself to look into the mirror without flinching and running away.

Before the first meeting, honestly rate yourself on the ten leadership characteristics below, using a 1-to-5 scale, to help initiate the discussion with your mirror. The questions can be customized as your career evolves.

1. How defensive do I get when someone challenges my stance?
Answer calmly and rationally = 1   Angrily confront the challenger = 5

1   2   3   4   5

2. How often do I let a team member finish what she wants to say before I respond?
Always allow to complete thought = 1   Always interrupt = 5

1   2   3   4   5

3. Who announces our team's breakthroughs?
The genius who made the breakthrough = 1   I do = 5

1   2   3   4   5

4. Would I positively recommend a genius on my team for a promotion that would take him away from my team?
The genius's career is more important than my own = 1   My success is more important = 5

1   2   3   4   5

5. How often does our team review project outcomes?
Always = 1   Never = 5

1   2   3   4   5

6. What is the goal of that review?
Review assumptions and process = 1   Define who is responsible for success or failure = 5

1   2   3   4   5

7. Could any given team member name our most important values?
Everyone could list our key values = 1   No one could = 5

1   2   3   4   5

8. Would I deceive my team if it resulted in a raise for me?
Never = 1   It depends on the raise = 5

1   2   3   4   5

9. Can team members name our top goals?
Everyone could name the goals = 1   No one could = 5

1   2   3   4   5

10. How often does the team come back to me for added resources needed to reach our goals?
Rarely = 1   Commonly = 5

1   2   3   4   5

Without telling your mirror how you rated yourself, ask her to rate you on each of these questions, then compare your answers to hers. There are two parts to this analysis. The first part of the discussion should be on the questions for which both you and your mirror rated you as a 4 or 5. These are weaknesses you need to improve. Center the discussion on concrete examples of past mistakes and alternative responses that could have led to better outcomes.

The second part of the discussion is more important. Focus on the questions for which your mirror rated you as a 4 or a 5, and you rated yourself as a 1 or 2. These areas are like warts on your back. They are there, but you cannot see them without a mirror. They are weaknesses you are not aware you have. They are the blind spots that can lead you to make mistakes.

Just realizing your unseen weaknesses is not enough to change. You have to recognize how much it costs you to hold them. Think back on your worst outcomes during the past few years and assess whether the areas in which your mirror rated you weak led you to make a wrong decision. The key to overcoming these weaknesses is to put an expensive price tag on them, one you are not willing to pay. If you can tag the unseen weakness with a specific failure, then it might become too expensive for you to keep.

The first time I did this with a colleague serving as my mirror, it was more painful than I thought it would be. I had rated myself as a very good listener, and one who deferred credit to others. My mirror thought I cut people off during discussions to make my own points, and that I liked to take personal credit for team achievements. Since I did not see myself this way, it forced me to change my internal image of myself, which was hard. It took a long time, but I like to think that I am better in both of these areas.

Work not only to rid yourself of your weaknesses, but also to build on qualities you want to foster. As you continue to meet with your mirror, discuss whether your changes achieved what you had hoped. If you got what you wanted from the changes, then you will want to continue the behavior and repeat the process. The idea is to repeat the process of self-analysis and make changes to reach your objective. Those initial ten questions can be expanded or altered to be more relevant to your situation as the process continues.

Focus on what you desire from a characteristic you are trying to add to your leadership. The objective for iterative self-correction is to be responsive to what your team needs from you to achieve greatness. The best self-assessment can identify problems, and the best self-correction can prevent them from becoming catastrophes. The reason you self-assess is to become a better fit with your team in order to make them more creative.

CRUCIAL TAKE-AWAY

If the same problems keep reoccurring, the problem is you.

RULE 2:
GET OUT OF THE WAY

4

The single biggest barrier to the productivity of geniuses is you. Leaders of geniuses are usually not even aware that they get in the way of the geniuses they lead. Leaders tend to think they contribute much more than they actually do. It makes them feel better about themselves.

When envisioning myself as a leader, I used to think I was like the director of a busy train station, switching trains from track to track to get them in and out on time. It took me years to understand that I was trying to direct the trains by standing in the middle of the tracks. I wanted to be in the center of everything. I was running up and down the tracks, waving my arms around, shouting to be heard as trains roared by in all directions, some jumping off the tracks to avoid hitting me.

This type of leadership is a losing proposition. If you succeed at forcing a direction on a genius, the new route will derail her thought process, and she will become passive and lose initiative. Or, if you fail at guiding geniuses, the speed of their thought processes will run over you, and they may fail to meet team goals. Too little guidance and too much both harm the productivity of the genius.

Einstein Goes to Washington

As the date for Einstein's arrival in the United States approached, Flexner became increasingly nervous. Einstein was concluding a promised appearance at Oxford University, whose faculty were trying to convince Einstein to remain in England. While in Europe, Einstein had been an outspoken critic of the growing anti-Semitism in Germany. In response, the Nazis seized his home, and German physicists started a campaign against his theories of relativity. Word came out of Germany that the Nazis might try to assassinate him. While in England, Einstein had his own undercover security detail.

Flexner was anxious about the German threats to Einstein's life. He may have been even more nervous that Einstein would be convinced to spend significant time at other universities. Louis Bamberger, the IAS board chair, began sending Flexner newspaper clippings of job offers extended to Einstein. Flexner was also concerned that Einstein's growing fame would politicize the scholarly retreat he was trying to create at the IAS.

The mayor of New York had planned a huge reception at the pier at which Einstein's ship was supposed to dock. There was even a marching band to welcome Einstein to the United States. The mayor was hungry for the media attention in an election year. The mayor, the band, journalists, and a crowd of curious onlookers waited for Einstein to disembark. When the last of the passengers emerged, there was no Einstein.

Flexner had arranged for a tugboat to pull up alongside the ocean liner in the harbor to sneak Einstein and his wife into New York. By the time the ship arrived in port, Einstein was already in Princeton eating ice cream at a soda shop and exploring his new surroundings. The crowd and the mayor went home disappointed.

Flexner's goal was to eliminate all the distractions that would inhibit his geniuses from making great advances. When the *New York Times* first ran the story about the establishment of the IAS, Flexner pleaded with the editor not to say much about him. He was not like Steve Jobs introducing the next Apple breakthrough in a huge news conference. Flexner wanted the focus of the story to be on Einstein and the Institute. Flexner saw himself positioned in the background removing obstacles and limiting distractions, a good role model for all leaders of genius.

However, Flexner went too far in trying to control Einstein's environment, and he almost lost Einstein. Believing he knew what was best for his distinguished recruit, Flexner began systematically declining all invitations for Einstein. Flexner worried that Einstein could not be trusted to handle his own public appearances, so he tried to manage Einstein's schedule. Flexner even turned down an invitation to the White House to dine with President Roosevelt. Flexner did not tell Einstein about the invitation. When Einstein found out what his boss had done, he was livid. Einstein went to the IAS board and threatened to quit if Flexner did not stop "meddling" in his personal affairs. Flexner backed down and worked to mend the relationship. He had gotten in the way, and it almost caused Einstein to leave the IAS.

Permitting New Approaches

When it came to research, Flexner was unafraid to support new approaches to old problems. He encouraged new fields, for which the questions had not yet even been articulated. Just as he had not interfered with John von Neumann when he was tinkering in the basement to build an early computer, he allowed others to follow their curiosity.

When the IAS economist Winfield Riefler wanted to apply statistics to economic data to predict future trends, other economists laughed at him. Economics at the time was more like philosophy or psychology, based on principles of individual human behavior. Riefler observed that population data was more accurate than summing up data from a few individuals. He found that trends that did not look significant on the surface could be important when analyzed closely using statistics. The federal government used Riefler's analytic technique extensively during World War II to fund the war effort. The technique not only helped win the war, but later was used in predicting Social Security budgets.

Flexner supported Riefler's efforts, and this approach is now a standard in economic analysis. Flexner fostered a culture of curiosity and interdisciplinary collaboration. When his faculty wanted to try something new or was excited about a new idea, he was able to get out of their way.

Indeed, Flexner did more than just get out of the way of these scientists. He actively encouraged nontraditional collaborations between unrelated disciplines and promoted innovative approaches, because this was exactly how he envisioned the IAS.

Align Authority with Responsibility

There is more to getting out of the way than simply encouraging new approaches. To be unobstructive, a leader must be able to hand over authority for the project. A leader should never assign responsibility for a project without providing the authority needed to fulfill that responsibility. In my experience, this is a common error in leading geniuses. Even when we are on guard against it, we still do it. Leaders by nature hoard power, often subconsciously.

This Rule is essential for the success of any project. One survey of 500 managers found that lack of authority is a major contributor to project failure. Giving geniuses ownership of the project means aligning authority with responsibility. Unless a genius feels that he owns the project, he will not feel free to throw himself into his work. A genius must be able to make decisions that alter the direction of the project. He must be able to decide on resources, infrastructure, and experiments. The other side to this coin is that having authority means that a genius is also held accountable for the goals of the project.

A classic example of letting employees own their work is FedEx. The company allows every driver to choose the best route for delivering packages. This freedom provides an additional layer of local knowledge over GPS directions and often results in saving time. The practice resulted in a measurable increase in job satisfaction and employee retention.

Rebellion or Apathy

If you want to fail as a leader, just give your team a difficult problem, and then restrict their ability to test their ideas on how to solve it. The more difficult the project, the more important it is that your smartest team members can fully utilize their intelligence.

You may not know you are hoarding authority until one of two things happens: an all-out rebellion like the team at Shockley Semiconductor or the bored apathy of the middle managers at Kodak. Whenever I see a team rebel or become apathetic, I know that the leader has assigned responsibility without authority. Team members can rebel and try to oust the leader or they can leave for another company. If they leave, they may try to destroy the team on the way out the door. Alternatively, the genius could learn helplessness, which leads to apathy. This is even worse than all-out rebellion, because she will stay and draw a paycheck without doing anything productive. Time on social media goes way up, hallway discussions are more about the college basketball playoffs than new computer algorithms, and innovation disappears.

Withholding power can cause bitterness and victimhood. When geniuses see that they cannot reach the goal with the authority provided, they begin to see the job as unfair. They see you as the major barrier but cannot do anything about it. When a rat is given a negative experience, say a mild electrical shock they cannot avoid, it just lies there unmoving. This is called "learned helplessness." This is the same as a genius who cannot leave her job because she needs the money. She feels blocked from solving the problems before her, but cannot change jobs, so she learns helplessness.

Warning Signs of Hoarding Authority

So how can you recognize when you are hoarding power and resources, and stifling creativity and productivity? If you are self-aware, there are warning signs that come early enough to allow you to get out of the way of creativity. You are hoarding authority when:

- **You insist on discussing every experiment.** You think the team needs your constant involvement. You want to discuss every task, no matter how small, and not just overall project goals. You become a bottleneck in the project. Nothing can be done without meeting with you.

- **You demand micro-approval, which means you have to approve every detail of the project.** The genius has to come back again and again for approvals every step of the way. Micro-approvals increase control over the genius. Often, this type of leader enjoys cutting off efforts by claiming that they were never approved and keeps the genius guessing what was actually approved. This manipulation generates team fear and leads to a massive suppression of creativity.

This type of leadership has additional drawbacks. Requiring micro-approvals makes you incredibly busy and makes you feel needed, which is a self-esteem booster. Because you have made yourself so busy, things can sit for weeks waiting for your approval. You slow geniuses down, frustrating them. You may do this without consciously realizing it and would probably deny it.

A leader is not the best person to decide what needs to be purchased or what experiments need to be done. The person who is doing the work can make a more informed decision than you can. You will have difficulty holding geniuses accountable if you do not provide what they need, because not having authority gives them an excuse for failure.

- **Your metrics of success for the genius are vague.** Your expectations are vague, because you want the right to change them and avoid responsibility for failure. You want to maintain control of the genius's progress, and you want to define success yourself. Not communicating metrics for success is a sure sign that you do not trust the genius or yourself to make the grade. Worse, you may not have a clue about what success looks like.

The first thing every strong team does at the start of any project is to define measurable outcomes of success. You should be leading this conversation and not preventing it.

■ *You do not give clear feedback in real time.* This feedback should be more about encouragement than criticism and more about process than micro-approving direction. Your job is to set goals but not to define each step on the way to those goals. When a genius is functioning well, let him know that his process is beautiful, even if he is not making much progress. You should celebrate a successful process just as much as a successful achievement.

Results still matter, and you are what your record is, as the football coach Bill Parcells famously said. If the right process is in place, there will be progress. When the genius's process becomes flawed, focus on how to improve it and not what went wrong.

■ *You routinely celebrate your own achievements rather than the achievements of others.* The biotech giant Biogen had a wall of plaques with all the company's patents and the names of the scientists who made the discoveries behind the patents. Each time a new patent was granted, they served champagne and hung the plaque. The scientists receiving the patent rang a large bell that echoed through the hallways, so everyone would know what had happened.

"When the bell rang, we would all come out of our labs and offices," explained Burt Adelman, former chief scientific officer for Biogen, to me, "and congregate at the wall to celebrate the patent. It reminded us that we were making progress. We were succeeding."

■ *You make your team operate on your schedule and not theirs.* You call meetings frequently, at their most productive times of the day, and the meetings are long. As a leader, you have to ensure that your team's geniuses have time to concentrate on the problems of the project. If you drop in at odd hours for impromptu discussions, they will be flattered, but less productive. The leader needs to streamline workflow and not constantly interrupt it.

- *You rarely ask for real time input on the project.* Feedback can threaten you, because it can call your leadership into question. You may not even realize that you avoid asking for feedback on any decisions. You use your meetings with your team to convey information about a decision already made, not to discuss a decision before it is made.

- *You create a climate of fear on the team.* If there is more fear of failure than joy at success, you are maintaining control by punishing any deviation from the path you have laid down. Ruling through fear is a classic totalitarian leadership style. It keeps you in control of the team. If you are an authoritarian leader, your team will never be honest about their progress, and they will never take risky leaps of creativity to make technological breakthroughs.

  You can generate a climate of fear in subtle ways. Simply becoming angry at the expenses for an experiment can make a genius afraid to approach you about an innovation. You may be creating a climate of fear without realizing it. The best and brightest of your team will leave, and it is rare that such a team leader will achieve anything.

Five Obstacles to Delegating Power

Why do leaders hoard power and fail to listen to input? They do this even when they know that innovation occurs best when there is freedom to pursue the project creatively. There are five reasons why you may fail to delegate authority:

1. **You are insecure about your ability to lead genius.** When you do not trust yourself, it is difficult to trust your team. The geniuses on your team quickly perceive that you do not trust them without

realizing your mistrust is really a lack of confidence in yourself. An insecure leader cannot listen creatively, because this type of listening involves giving up control of the conversation and even the topic. You may not be aware you are hoarding power. You believe the team needs you or it will fail. This feeling of being indispensable is important for your self-esteem. I have even seen a leader invent an emergency in which he is needed to intervene. The leader picks an insignificant issue and blows it out of proportion, and then jumps in and gives instructions on how to face this "emergency."

2. **You do not want to train anyone to lead a project.** It takes time to train a genius to lead. Often by the time you train someone to perform a given task, the need for that task is over. You might as well have done it yourself. Although training a new leader takes time, in the end it increases productivity far more than the time invested. A trained genius can perform the task many times later, and you will never have to do it again.

You might convince yourself that you can do the task better. This is a dangerous syndrome. When you start thinking you are irreplaceable, thinking that only you can make correct decisions soon follows. If you think that only you can make correct decisions, it becomes impossible for anyone to suggest better alternatives. You stop self-assessing, and your intrinsic biases will imprison the creativity of the genius.

If a project has the potential to be spectacularly successful, a leader can fear losing credit if she delegates too much. I have seen brilliant scientists begin their careers working together as friends, then become bitter enemies when the project succeeds. Roger Guillemin and Andrew Schally, two scientists who first isolated the brain proteins that control the release of thyroid and gonadal hormones, were friends and collaborators at the start of their project. As the project drew attention and there was talk of a Nobel Prize, they split into two warring laboratories, each afraid the other was stealing their data. Both were awarded the Nobel Prize in 1977.

3. **You really like doing the job you are going to give away.** In this case, you will be giving away one of the reasons you go to work. In one of my leadership positions, I had to turn over direct authority for running a program in my own area of expertise to one of my division chiefs. I was completely confident in his abilities to manage the program, but I liked doing it, too. It was with a sense of loss that I no longer ran that service line. It took me several years to get out of the way and let him do his job.

   The way I handled the situation was to meet more often with that division chief and listen to how the program was going. I tried not to offer opinions on every situation. At those meetings, I got to bask in the same feeling I had when I was supervising the program. Then I left him alone.

4. **Resources are limited.** This obstacle may be out of your control, and you must learn to accept the limitations of your environment. If you lack resources, you must carefully shepherd funding and infrastructure. You and your geniuses must prioritize every expenditure and experiment. Your team cannot build every prototype they want and do every experiment.

   When resources are scarce, delegating the selection of direction to a genius is even more difficult for a leader, because he will be held responsible for the outcomes. Transferring power remains the best way to enhance the creativity of a genius even in this situation.

5. **The lines of authority above you are blurred.** This blurring of authority may result in contradictory instructions. When you ask for clarification, the confusion may get worse. You cannot delegate authority, because you are not sure what the goals are.

If this happens, it is possible that two of your superiors are battling for control of the organization. You can easily become a common enemy and a focal point of their enmity. They will enjoy a short truce while they finish you off, and then turn on each other again. In this situation, you need to explicitly document your team's goals to both superiors, so that your intentions are never in question.

Leading When Your Own Authority Is Restricted

Sometimes your superior might limit your authority on a project to the extent that it is difficult to complete the assignment. For example, you may be given leadership of a team for which you cannot hire or fire anyone. You are only a glorified advisor.

A superior, who has been promoted above his intelligence and knows it, can restrict your authority. Unless your boss is superb at self-reflection and self-correction, he will be insecure and will spend most of his effort protecting himself. Your incentive or even your position may depend on your team's completion of the project, but you have no hire/fire power, no signatory authority over resources, or cannot even evaluate the team members annually.

You do have one advantage. You lead a team of genius. They respond much better to mutual commitment to an important project than to being obedient. To excel, they need to be intrinsically motivated and highly creative, two characteristics that do not depend on whether you have authority. Your commitment to the team and your engagement with the project is what they need. The innovation of genius can overcome the restrictions your supervisor has placed on your authority.

Motivation can be complicated, because in these situations you often do not have the ability to reward or terminate a team member. You cannot threaten any consequences, because it is unlikely you can implement those consequences. If you resort to such threats, you will quickly lose credibility as a leader. Identifying and articulating shared goals and explaining the logical reasons for taking action can make it possible to alter your team's course of action when your authority is limited.

What Does Delegating Look Like?

One of the many signs of a genius is that he can make connections others do not see. This conceptual convergence can only occur when the genius is free to make those connections.

Kary Mullis, who conceived of the polymerase chain reaction (PCR), worked at Cetus, a small biotech firm in San Diego, which gave him the freedom to test whether PCR would work or not. They did not regiment his time, ration his supplies, or review each of his experiments. What Cetus and many of the other small biotech firms of the '80s did well was delegate experimental authority to their genius employees. Because of this freedom, Cetus gained the first patents on PCR, which Cetus eventually sold to Hoffman-LaRoche for $300 million.

The deal was good for both corporations. It saved Cetus from bankruptcy and that price was a bargain for such a revolutionary technology. Hoffman-LaRoche made an estimated $2 billion in royalties in just a few years and created a new instrumentation unit for PCR equipment, which also made strong profits. Many years later, when Mullis won the Nobel Prize, he said, "I will take it!"[1] He thought that it was about time he won.

Trusting Genius

Turning over authority for a given project is a remarkable demonstration of trust. Being able to let go of authority and get out of the way of a genius are based on trust. If you trust the intellect and character of a genius, if you trust that the genius will not abuse the power and will get the job done, it is easy to let go of power. Given this proof of trust, it is likely that a genius will feel more responsible for the project and will work harder. If you are uneasy about transferring authority, then you either mistrust yourself, or you have hired the wrong people.

Trust is the foundation of the relationship between you and a genius. You must trust geniuses to be creative. When geniuses feel more in control of their work environment, they are more open to stretch goals and new initiatives. You can introduce new avenues to explore without overwhelming them.

In the end, getting out of the way benefits you. You can gain far more than you lose when you transfer ownership of a task to a genius and get out of the way. Unimaginable discoveries occur because a genius is in control of her own destiny and is free to think. Every genius is at heart still a kid with his first Lego set. Do not ration the Legos. The wonder of a new discovery and the sense of play drive a genius more than you think. The transfer of authority is not as helpful in leading people who are not geniuses. Most employees need clear directions and strict guidelines for their effort.

The diagram shown in Figure 4.1 (next page) demonstrates how a leader, who does not trust himself, imprisons the genius on the team. When leaders do not self-assess and self-correct, they begin to mistrust themselves. If members of your team are much smarter than you, you can feel insecure. Your shortcomings compared to their brilliance will be on display daily. To maintain an internal image of yourself that you deserve to lead because of your innate ability, you must deceive yourself.

As Figure 4.1 shows, when a leader is insecure, he can behave in ways that imprison the genius on his team.

The self-assessing leader transfers ownership of the project to the genius. This can only happen if the leader trusts himself. Confidence increases his ability to transfer authority to the genius and get out of the way, which demonstrates that the leader trusts the genius. When geniuses own the project, they are not working for just a paycheck, but because they believe in the wider significance of the goals of the project. Having the trust of their leader frees the genius to be fully creative.

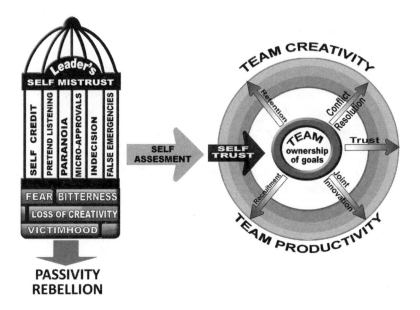

When geniuses are excited about their work, it leads to better recruitment and retention. The entire team trusts each other more, because their shared purpose means they care about the same values. Sharing values makes it easier to find common ground in a dispute and leads to more efficient conflict resolution. Improving recruitment, retention, conflict resolution, and most importantly, the feeling of being trusted, leads to far greater productivity than if you imprison your genius with your own self-doubt.

CRUCIAL TAKE-AWAY:

You can only trust a genius if you trust yourself.

RULE 3:
SHUT UP AND LISTEN

5

The revolution in technology, the very reason there is a proliferation of teams of genius in most companies, has created a multitude of new ways to communicate. We live wrapped up in our mobile devices, with emails, texts, video, and Internet drop boxes. This means that the amount of noise in our world has multiplied exponentially.

The problem is greater than all the external noise coming at us. We are much more interested in communicating our thoughts than in hearing someone else's. This is especially true for leaders. Even when hearing someone else speak, leaders are not listening.

The single best way to get out of the way of your genius and fulfill Rule 2 is to shut up and listen. The very act of listening with your whole mind means that you have given up authority to another. You have quieted the noise inside your head. Listening turns out to be among the hardest things a leader will ever learn to do.

Listening to What Is Meant

In 1937, two members of the IAS board, Samuel Leidesdorf and Herbert Maass, complained to Flexner about the anti-Semitism at Princeton. Both men had sons who had been denied admission to Princeton, probably because they were Jewish. Jewish faculty members at the IAS, who agreed that the anti-Semitism at Princeton was outrageous, had also approached these board members. Maass and

Leidesdorf recommended that the ties of the IAS with Princeton be weakened. They suggested that the entire mathematics faculty move out of the building they shared with Princeton and into the new Fuld Hall, which the IAS owned. They also wanted the faculty to have more say in the decisions the IAS made, because Flexner was blind to Princeton's religious prejudice.

Flexner's initial reaction was incredulity at the claims. He acknowledged that there might be isolated instances of anti-Semitism at Princeton, but he did not think there was widespread systematic discrimination. Flexner was very sensitive about his relationship with Princeton, because he had hired away two of its most promising mathematicians, Oswald Veblen and James Alexander, in order to found the IAS School of Mathematics.

What Flexner failed to understand was that these complaints were not just about anti-Semitism. They were more about the overall viability of the IAS. Given that Flexner continued to spend money on new faculty and extraneous archaeological digs, the faculty worried about their own jobs and pensions. They wanted the IAS to be less dependent on Princeton, because they wanted the IAS to be more stable on its own. Flexner heard the complaints about anti-Semitism at Princeton, but he did not grasp what was behind them.

A year later, the faculty again came to Flexner asking for more representation on the IAS board, more voice in faculty appointments, and a say in the selection of the next director. In a meeting with the full faculty, the mathematician James Alexander claimed that the anti-Semitism at Princeton was the reason the mathematics faculty wanted to move to the new Fuld Hall.

This public claim upset Flexner, partly because he appreciated the help Princeton had extended to the IAS in its early days and did not want to risk ruining the relationship. In addition, the charge was personal, implying Flexner was ignoring and enabling this discrimination. Flexner responded by declaring there would no longer be faculty meetings and denying the request for increased faculty representation on the board.

The underlying reason for making that claim was that the faculty wanted more control over the administration of the IAS. They were afraid that Flexner was going to bankrupt the IAS, and they would be out of their jobs. It was a way for them to bring attention to what they really wanted. Instead of taking the time to listen and understand what his faculty were trying to tell him, Flexner grasped only the charge of anti-Semitism at Princeton, which was likely real, but not the root cause of the dispute.

There is a difference between hearing someone speak and truly listening to her. Flexner heard the words but did not grasp the significance of what was said. We tend to catalogue words without cross-referencing them or putting them in context. The implications of what the faculty said eluded Flexner.

The faculty rebelled against Flexner's leadership. They wrote letters of complaint to the Bambergers and other board members. Within a year, they succeeded in ousting Flexner as director of the Institute.

The Cost of Not Listening

Business schools teach many case histories of catastrophic financial failure that could have been avoided if the CEO had truly listened. The *New York Times* asked Steve Sasson, the engineer at Kodak who invented the first digital camera in 1975, how it went when he presented the idea to senior Kodak management.

"It was filmless photography, so management's reaction was, 'that's cute—but don't tell anyone about it'," he said.[1] Kodak was so afraid that it would cannibalize their film revenue that they buried it. They were right, digital photography did end up eating the entire film industry.

This is not the end of the poor decisions at Kodak that came from ignoring their own engineers, who were decades ahead of their time. In 1996, twenty-one years later, when they finally got around to using their own digital photographic technology, they created the Advantix system at the cost of $500 million. This system allowed photographers to preview their shots and pick the ones they wanted to print. Advantix essentially was a digital camera that still required the user to print photographs. Kodak spent half a billion dollars to force a new technology into an old model, in order to save the company's film revenue.

Of course, it failed. Why would anyone buy a digital camera and still pay for film and prints? Kodak leadership heard the presentations of its engineers, but did not hear what the words meant. The company's sense of self-preservation ended up being greater than its ability to recognize innovation, and that killed the company. If a current business plan relies on a technology staying the same, that company is in grave danger.

Blockbuster is another example of a CEO's failure to listen, which led to a mammoth bankruptcy. Reed Hastings, the co-founder of Netflix, tried to get Blockbuster CEO John Antioco to buy his company for $50 million. Former Netflix CFO Barry McCarthy remembered flying down to Texas with Hastings and other Netflix leaders to meet with Antioco and his staff.

"Reed . . . proposed to them that we run their brand online and that they run [our] brand in the stores," McCarthy said, "and they just about laughed us out of their office."[2]

Blockbuster executives thought Netflix had a niche business, not a market-disrupting new technology. They bet their company that the new technology would not hurt their business, and they were wrong. The founders and executives of Blockbuster cashed out much of their equity and diversified before its failure. The thousands of employees and small investors were the losers of this bet. One reason leaders do not listen to their team is that there are often few consequences for failure.

Blockbuster eventually decided to pursue Internet movies on demand, but chose to partner with—believe it or not—Enron. Blockbuster signed a twenty-year deal with Enron's telecommunications arm, only to cancel the contract when Enron started its death spiral nine months later.

Netflix had a revolutionary business model, which made Blockbuster obsolete, but Antioco did not understand the implications of what Hastings had proposed. He simply did not listen. The result of his failure to understand the model was that Blockbuster went through bankruptcy years ago and Netflix's market capitalization was about $19 billion in 2015.

Classic business analysis of Kodak and Blockbuster shows that they had one good idea. When their foundational technology became obsolete, they were unable to change, because they cherished their one victory. I suggest that their failure came because their leaders did not listen to other good ideas.

All the noise in the world makes it much easier to listen to yourself and ignore all external communication. You can convince yourself that you have heard your clients' desires and met their specifications, but you may not have really listened to what they were saying. If you just keep repeating what you want them to say often enough in your own mind, it becomes your reality. You think they have really said what you think you heard, because you have said it to yourself so many times. This is made worse by hubris. You begin thinking you know what is best for your clients, not because you have listened to them, but because of your position as a leader.

Why Leaders Do Not Listen

Perhaps at the most fundamental level we do not listen to one another because we think we can read another's mind. We think we know what someone is going to say before he says it. One study has shown that people routinely overestimate how well they know what another person is thinking.[3] They impute their own knowledge to the other person. Not only did the participants in this study misunderstand what the other person was thinking, but they were not aware that they misunderstood.

We misunderstand what others are thinking, because we fail to realize they have separate minds from us. We think we know what someone will say before she says it, because we assume she will say what we would say.

The Space Shuttle *Challenger* disaster was a horrific example of a failure to listen. Engineers relayed their anxiety about the defective O-rings around the engine to the mission leaders, but the mission leaders categorized the warning as typical pre-mission nervousness. The O-rings leaked during takeoff and the fuel exploded, killing all seven people aboard. The engineers were an alternative voice, saying something awkward and unpopular, which was subordinated by the mission leaders. "One of the reasons [for not listening] was the power dynamics between the people giving that information and the people who were in charge of the situation," Kelley See, an assistant professor at the New York University School of Business, said to *Forbes*.[4]

See's rationale for leaders not listening is similar to the concept of subordinated alternatives, *subaltern* for short, which is used in the study of history. This theory states that novel ideas usually are given less weight than current paradigms in order to maintain the status quo. The new ideas become subordinated alternatives. Subaltern historians point out how difficult it is for people to hear ideas outside of their expectations. When presented with information that does not directly fit current cultural or economic perspectives, people find it extremely difficult to hear a person out. When an innovative speaker reaches the boundary of our expectations, we will often stop listening. If we listen to a subaltern voice, we often warp his or her narrative to fit into our prevailing expectations. Only after tragedy strikes us do we give the subaltern voice enough consideration to see that it differs from what we perceived.

Power Trumps Expertise

Subordination of alternative voices is common in organizations today. Leaders often discredit innovative concepts by placing them into categories of ideas that have failed or are already in place. Leaders do this for several reasons. By categorizing the idea, they assume power over it and retain their authority. Some leaders are uncomfortable with an idea they do not understand. They categorize innovation as the status quo in order to convince themselves that they really understand it. Finally, some leaders are complacent, and implementing a novel concept requires hard work.

The difference in power between a leader and a genius can make a leader give the words of the genius less weight. Studies have found that simply having power makes a leader less likely to listen. Powerful leaders routinely ignore advice from novices and experts alike. They tend to do this because they are overconfident in their own judgment, and they feel competitive with the advice giver. They worry that innovation originating from someone below them will prove that they are unnecessary and could lead to their replacement.

The same study also showed that both novices and experts, who feel that they have little power, carefully weigh advice from all others, but give the most credence to the advice of someone they perceive as powerful, whether or not that person has expertise in the area.[5] The perception of power trumps the perception of expertise.

Talking Over Each Other

With the potential consequences of not listening, you might wonder why leaders do not work at listening better. One reason is that the more power a leader has, the less punishment he risks for being wrong. Powerful leaders are less likely to be persuaded by the ideas of others. According to another study on listening, powerful leaders do not pay attention to what others are thinking, because they do not want to feel constrained in their decision making.[6] They see no reason for them to try to understand what their team thinks. They don't care, because there are no consequences.

Having power in an organization can induce a leader to make snap decisions without obtaining input from experts, because being wrong has less consequence to a powerful leader. For the most powerful leaders, there is less motivation to gather data for any decision and to listen carefully to what others say about the decision. As long as the organization survives, powerful executives can reduce the consequences of their bad decisions simply by being in power. The point may come, however, when no amount of power can reverse the effects of a bad decision.

The higher an executive is, the worse the decisions can be before consequences occur. The weight of bad decisions that result from not listening can ultimately destroy a leader's power base. This can mean the death of that organization.

If simply being a leader puts you at risk for not listening, you need to have strategies to avoid the trap. The study that found power can make leaders deaf to the thoughts of others included a final experiment that indicates we can learn to listen better. When the researchers induced a feeling of cooperation between the powerful leader and those giving advice, the leader was more likely to listen to the advice.

In the end, all those stupid team-building exercises at the company retreat may not have been so stupid after all. When you have a cooperative tone, you set an example for the geniuses who work for you. When they are committed as part of a team, they will listen more.

A good leader sets up a formal process in which everyone listens more, and the best ideas win. A great leader can get a room full of geniuses to do that.

How Can You Tell If You Are Not Listening?

I use several methods to prevent myself from not listening. I take notes during almost all scheduled conversations. This has become easier with the advent of tablets, which I carry into all meetings.

The quality of my notes indicates how well I listened. I email these notes to myself and store them under my schedule, so that I can rapidly access the main points discussed in any meeting. I am amazed at how many times my memory of a verbal agreement is skewed more in my favor than in the other person's. The written notes keep me honest.

Asking thoughtful questions is a crucial aspect to listening well. Some pauses are a good sign. The silence means that people are thinking about what was said and do not have an automatic reply. A fast-paced conversation without any silence can seem exciting, but it may not be the most effective way to communicate ideas. Rapid-fire conversations tend to be superficial. In order to hear what someone is saying, you have to pause to take it in before you can respond thoughtfully.

If you are thinking about your reply before another has finished speaking, then you know that you are not really listening. You are faking participation in the conversation by using Terminator-like automated responses to avoid expending the greater amount of energy it takes to concentrate on what the other person is saying.

Perhaps the best way you can tell if you have listened well is whether you do something based on the discussion. Acting on the advice of your team is a very effective team-building exercise. When you act on advice, you demonstrate that you heard what was said, and it made a difference. Changing your direction because of the input of a genius is a compelling way to empower that genius.

Methods of Listening

We have all become adept at faking conversations. The spectrum of listening ranges from total nonparticipation to an active give and take from which both participants benefit. Inspired by *The Art of Managing People* by Phillip Hunsaker and Anthony Alessandra, I have modified the four categories of listeners to make them more relevant to leading genius.[7] They are the Non-Listener, the Pretend Listener, the Transactional Listener, and the Creative Listener.

The Non-Listener

Non-listeners hold conversations with themselves. The speaker might as well not be present. The motivation for this type of listener is to gain self-esteem from the conversation, and non-listeners do not care what the other person gets out of the exchange. They frequently interrupt, changing the subject to one that features them. They often leave abruptly and want the last word when they do. The more leaders hoard power, and the longer they have it, the more likely they are to fall into this category. Leaders who have been in the same position for many years cannot realize they are not listening.

The Pretend Listener

Pretend listeners only engage a small fraction of their brains during a conversation. They can say ridiculous and nonsensical things during a conversation, because they are not really engaged. Most of their attention is on something more attractive, such as an upcoming vacation to Barcelona. Pretend listeners nod agreeably and interject automatic words of encouragement.

This type of listener is on autopilot, but their attention can suddenly shift back to the conversation if a word or phrase catches their attention, "bonus," or "promotion," for example. They listen selectively to the conversation and commonly misinterpret what was said. They can swear they heard you make a commitment you did not.

The Transactional Listener

Most of us fall into the third category of listener, the transactional listener. We will listen carefully if we expect to get something out of it. We listen to what is being said and judge the content without connecting with the speaker. We participate in the conversation, but only on our own terms. We form opinions on what we thought was meant, rather than on the speaker's intent.

We are exchanging time for information with this type of listening, but no more than necessary. We want to gain something from the conversation. If there is give and take, it is because we are transacting a subconscious deal, trading personal effort for the speaker's information. This type of listener is ambitious and may not be as committed to the genius as it seems.

The Creative Listener

The creative listener can discover innovation in any conversation. They add value to the speaker. They are fully engaged on the speaker's terms. They read body language. They look the speaker in the face, because that is the best gauge of how important the topic is to the speaker. They listen carefully to voice inflection and the nuance of word choice. They silently digest what is said before replying.

Their replies are thoughtful and unique, rather than automatic. The replies are not focused on themselves but are geared toward the speaker's thoughts on the topic. Their replies are encouraging and convey safety and comfort. This listener wants the speaker to be as open as possible in providing the best and most creative ideas on the topic.

Creative listeners get the most from conversations with geniuses on their team, because the geniuses are communicating on their own terms. The geniuses are free to express themselves and can be their most creative in that open space. Great ideas are birthed with this type of conversation.

My father co-discovered an equation that allowed space vehicles to reenter the atmosphere without burning up. He told me the idea came from a chance conversation with Lester Lees, a professor at the California Institute of Technology. They were talking about something unrelated to the reentry, when Lees said something that struck a chord in my father's mind. My father asked a tangential follow-up question, and another, until they had the outlines of the equation, because they listened creatively to each other.

Tools for Creative Listening

To lead genius, it is essential that you practice creative listening. If you use the following tools, you will connect with your geniuses.

- **Look directly at the speaker.** It is harder for your mind to wander when you are looking directly at someone. You can observe facial expressions and body language. Crossing arms or legs can mean that they are guarded and uncomfortable. It may mean that they disagree with you but are afraid to say it. The inability to look you in the eye can mean they are shading the truth or they are embarrassed by what they are saying. Alternatively, they could simply be socially awkward, which is common for a genius. It is important to pay close attention to people while they are speaking in order to know the difference.

- **Make the speaker as comfortable as possible.** Show the speaker you are listening, which communicates that you value her, and what she says is important to you. Since talking with you, the leader, can be anxiety provoking, especially for the socially awkward genius, use encouraging words and nod to help the speaker open up more. I suggest not sitting too close, keeping an open posture, and facing the speaker squarely without crossing your arms or legs. Reply in neutral or encouraging tones.

- **Provide reflective feedback.** At intervals in the conversation, reflect back a summary, such as "What I am hearing you say is. . . ." Also, ask questions that lead to more depth in the conversation, for example, "If that is true, then does it mean this?" Asking questions not only indicates you are listening, but it engages the genius to go a step further in his discussion. Your questions can open up new vistas and take the conversation into realms where creativity can flourish and boundaries can be crossed, to exciting new areas never before explored.

Encouraging with questions can stimulate participants to ping-pong crazy ideas back and forth. They begin deriving innovative solutions to perplexing problems on the fly, ratcheting up the energy, and making significant conceptual advances.

- ■ *Do not make a judgment on the worth of any idea.* Judgments discourage further discussion and kill creativity. Make sure the speaker has time to completely flesh out an idea before asking a summarizing question.

    Try not to interrupt. Silence is fine, because it makes you think about what was said and allows the speaker to get his thoughts in order.

If you use these tools when listening, you will convey respect for the other person. If you do not respect the speaker, the tools for creative listening will not work for you. At best, you will end up a transactional listener, assessing what is in the conversation for you.

Creative listening gives weight to the individual speaking. You are giving her your most precious commodity, your attention, because you think she is worth it. The operative word here is "giving." You are not trading your time for something of equal or greater value. The conversation is not conditional upon what you get out of it. The speaker is not anxious and hurried. She is free to make mistakes, and her greatest creativity will result from that freedom.

How Creative Listening Increases Productivity

If you become a creative listener, you can markedly increase the innovation of a genius. This type of participatory listening improves morale. When you ask for input and truly listen to what is said before making a decision, you promote ownership of the decision. A genius will feel responsible for the outcome of that decision, because he helped make it. This dynamic validates his intelligence, and makes him feel that he owns his future.

At a time when every company is searching for that one genius who can advance its technology, the more camaraderie you can build, the more likely a genius is to join the team for the long term. Creative listening improves recruitment and retention. I have found one of the most common reasons for leaving cited in our exit interviews is that faculty members did not feel that their supervisors listened to them. See Figure 5.1.

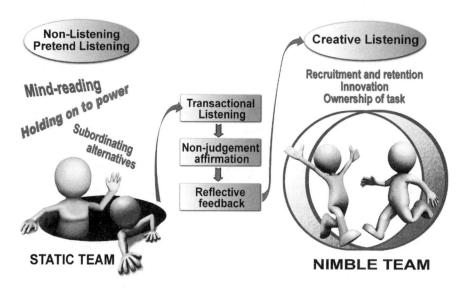

If an employee thinks that no one listens to her, she will stop presenting new ideas. She will isolate herself and stop interacting in a meaningful way. That employee's engagement with the team will be lost; her productivity will decrease, and that employee will become increasingly bitter.

A leader who listens carefully can forestall many conflicts. You serve as a steam valve: Just letting someone vent can prevent crisis. You also are the oil between the gears that prevents two geniuses from grinding against each other, with irritation flaring up to anger.

During a medical law course I took many decades ago, the attorney teaching it stated that the most common reason malpractice lawsuits went to trial was not the adverse medical outcome, but because the patients felt the physician did not listen to them. He went on to say that simply listening to patients describe their difficult experiences and suffering through it with them averted most of the planned litigation.

Physicians have a reputation for being notoriously bad listeners. Many health care errors occur because doctors do not listen to patients or to one another. We have worked hard in my department to practice creative listening. We work at listening not just to our patients but also to one another—during surgery, during a research experiment, or during a case presentation for a consult.

CRUCIAL TAKE-AWAY:

Get input from the geniuses a decision affects before making the decision. Then they will own the decision.

RULE 4:
TURN OVER THE ROCKS

6

"When you turn over rocks and look at all the squiggly things underneath, you can either put the rocks down, or you can say, 'My job is to turn over rocks and look at the squiggly things,'" Fred Purdue, former vice president at Pitney Bowes, once said to author Jim Collins.[1]

Turning over the rocks to let others see all the ugly creatures underneath is an essential foundation for leading exceptionally smart people, but it is easier said than done. It can be embarrassing, scary, and sometimes costly.

On the other hand, hiding information and deceiving others about decisions practically guarantees that these deceptions will become ghosts that haunt the future of your organization. Darkness makes things grow until they become too big to hide, and you cannot control what escapes. Many of the problems that occur with leading genius originate from secrecy and deception on the part of the leader.

The best way to avoid dysfunction in your team of geniuses is to let them see all the squirmy things in your head. Secrecy creates problems, and transparency solves them. Truth disarms any attacks against you and protects you from future recriminations. As the saying goes, "Sunshine is the best disinfectant."

Flexner's Squiggly Things

At the beginning of the IAS, Flexner was open and transparent in almost all of his decisions. He routinely consulted the faculty on all major decisions, especially on the next hire. He had no agenda that was hidden and personal. He often took his faculty's advice, because he recognized that he was not a scientist himself. He discussed all of the first hires with Einstein and took his advice religiously. He held regular faculty meetings, during which he discussed any new directions and aired any difficulties.

He often invited faculty to his summer cottage in Canada to spend time with him and his family. He had personal relationships with many members of the faculty, which increased transparent communication. At the beginning of the IAS, Flexner understood the importance of seeking out and listening to the advice of others. He sought input from many famous scientists around the country, and he spent hours asking the opinions of the first faculty hired for the IAS.

As the financial constraints of the Great Depression closed around the IAS, made worse by the Bambergers poor management of the endowment, Flexner stopped being transparent. By 1937, he was making decisions without asking anyone's advice, and his decisions took everyone by surprise. To make matters worse, he failed to explain to the faculty or the IAS board any of the reasons behind his decisions.

Oswald Veblen, the Chair of the Mathematics department, repeatedly pressed Flexner to build an IAS facility to house the mathematics department, so they could leave the building they shared with Princeton's mathematics faculty. Flexner denied his request without explaining the financial problems he was facing. One of the crucial problems he faced was the difficulty of convincing the Bamberger family to continue to support the IAS.

Veblen did not realize that Flexner was operating under such intense financial constraints, because Flexner never told him. Flexner may have thought that admitting to the pressing financial constraints

would demonstrate his weakness as a leader. In fact, not being transparent and disguising the financial troubles of the IAS weakened his
leadership far more.

This disagreement over where to house the faculty was one of
the early sources of dissatisfaction with Flexner's leadership, which
later bloomed into a full-fledged revolt. Veblen felt that Flexner was
not listening to him (Rule 3), because Flexner offered weak excuses
for denying Veblen's request and never explained the true rationale
behind his decision.

This lack of transparency surfaced once again when Flexner hired
several professors for the new school of economics at higher salaries
than others already on the faculty. Flexner had several preeminent
people in mind, whom he wanted to hire before he retired. He was
forced to choose between renowned economists and equitable salaries.

Rather than laying out the financial considerations for the board
and the faculty so that they understood his reasons, he tried to justify the inequity by pointing out that academic institutions in Europe
often had different salaries for the same position. His justification
sounded hollow to the faculty with lower salaries than their less senior
colleagues.

Flexner promised to make the salaries more equitable, but instead
hired even more faculty at higher salaries. One member of the board
sent out letters condemning the unequal salaries, which created an
uproar among the faculty, because all of the faculty were not aware
that there were two tiers of salaries. Some threatened to leave the
IAS, and others actively campaigned for Flexner's removal.

Trapped by Secret Agendas

Secret agendas can ensnare even a genius. Before World War II, Einstein became an international celebrity for his stands against German
Fascism. Several leading Communists sought to use him for their
own ends. By standing against Fascism, they tried to stand next to

Einstein and exploit his prestige for their own political ends. Doctored photos purporting to be Einstein visiting Soviet Russia were circulated by European Communist Parties, and rumors spread that he was a member of the Third International, the international arm of the Soviet Communist Party.

The avowed English Communist, Hewlett Johnson, offered Einstein his country home to work in, blithely ignoring the irony that a Communist should even own a country house. In his invitation, which was extended after Einstein had left Germany, Johnson lauded Einstein's "labors for peace," code words for peace through conversion of all nations to communism. If Einstein had accepted Johnson's offer, it would have been viewed as tacit approval of the English Communist Party.

Einstein also had supported a peace conference in Amsterdam, which was, unknown to him, organized by the Communist Party of the Netherlands. When the Communist support was pointed out to him, he responded, "I saw that it was a peace conference, and I did not concern myself with the organizer."[2]

Einstein became angry at the accusations that he was a member of the Communist Party, because he opposed totalitarianism in all forms. He wrote a letter to the *Times of London* and the *New York Times*, in which he said: "I have never had anything to do with the Third International, and have never been to Russia. Furthermore, it is manifest that the pictures purporting to be my photographs do not resemble me. The pictures are an attempted forgery inspired by political motives."[3]

The intense focus of geniuses often prohibits them from seeing how others use them for their own ends. Once geniuses discover they have been used, they are particularly angry and unforgiving.

The Cost of Deception

One discovered lie makes it difficult for anyone to trust you again. Worse, lies propagate themselves. Because they have no basis in reality, lies require a continuous effort to keep the truth hidden as time passes and perspectives change. Lies need new lies to keep the truth concealed. The lie moves in your organization like a tapeworm, sucking more and more energy from the team. Jeff Weiner, the CEO of LinkedIn, said, "I've come to learn there is a virtuous cycle to transparency and a very vicious cycle of obfuscation."[4] Lying takes more work and has far greater penalties than the truth.

When I asked 491 medical school departmental chairs from across the country what value they desired most from a leader, integrity between words and deeds was the most common answer. Genius needs to know that you tell them the truth and you keep your word.

Leadership by Chaos

In many organizations, leaders hoard information, because they see it as a source of power. Some leaders believe that secrecy ensures their own survival. Secrecy allows a leader to randomly change goals and create false emergencies, keeping genius off balance and maintaining power as the only person who understands the crisis. I call this leadership by chaos, and it disenfranchises genius and decreases productivity of the team.

Secrecy may give your detractors weapons to use against you. Transparency disarms dangerous situations, while deception raises the cost of any disagreement.

The chaotic leader must keep raising the stakes, or his team will catch on and begin to understand what is happening, which is how deception begets more deception. "Whoever is careless with the truth in small matters cannot be trusted with important matters," Einstein once said.[5]

The message here is not, "Don't get caught." With social media, federal Qui Tam whistleblower incentives, and phone videos, the chances that your secrets will be made public are high. WikiLeaks has proven that many times over, especially in the 2016 presidential election, where publication of Clinton campaign emails contained insults about her challenger for the nomination, Bernie Sanders. The message here is that deception is not worth the risk.

Pfizer agreed to pay $2.3 billion to settle allegations they deceptively marketed their painkiller Valdecoxib and three other medications. That cost does not include any regulatory fines that might come from settling litigation. There was evidence that Valdecoxib increased the risk of heart disease, but Pfizer covered that up in its marketing. They also secretly paid for trips to resorts for physicians to induce them to prescribe these medications.

The settlement was the largest ever for a U.S. corporation for deceptive marketing practices. Pfizer denied it, fought it, and the cost just kept getting bigger. They could have saved a huge amount of time and money by disclosing their errors and implementing a plan to prevent it from happening again. This settlement pales in comparison to the loss of half the value of Pfizer stock. The company's market cap fell by more than $100 billion during the litigation. They now face a long and costly shareholder lawsuit as well for alleged mismanagement of the firm during this time.

Money can make it tempting to be deceptive about certain data, especially when that data makes your product look bad, but deceptive practices cost more in the end. For example, in 1983 two Philip Morris scientists, Drs. Victor De Noble and Paul Mele, wanted to publish their finding that nicotine was addictive. Philip Morris not only prohibited them from publishing, but the company also buried their data, because the implications were terrifying for the business. The findings implied that nicotine made the smoker addicted to a delivery system that also contained cancer-causing tar. Their deliberate suppression of the truth was one of the justifications for a record settlement.

Given the invasion of social media and Internet search engines into almost every business activity, transparency exists whether or not you want it. We live in an unavoidable reputation economy, Clive Thompson proposed in *Wired* magazine, "Google is not a search engine. Google is a reputation-management system. And that's one of the most powerful reasons so many CEOs have become more transparent: Online, your rep is quantifiable, findable, and totally unavoidable."[6]

You might as well embrace this transparency. The externalities of your business—the spillover effects of your business on the environment and society at large—are unavoidable. Given the explosion of information technology, externalities can now be attached to your organization whether you think that attachment is correct or not.

Why were Pfizer and Philip Morris so secretive? The reason is that neither knew that externalities have become much more apparent to the public, and the public attaches them to a company and its product much more commonly.

The Revolution of Proactive Transparency

This chapter proposes something that is revolutionary among high technology organizations today, and that is being proactively transparent. Turn over the rocks without being asked. Predict what information is important and provide that information before being asked for it, and before any decision is made. Do not wait to be asked, and certainly do not wait for the subpoena.

Transparency goes against the Steve Jobs model of leadership. He demanded secrecy about what direction Apple was going next. Granted, the field of technology is highly competitive, but Steve Jobs was notoriously nontransparent with his own team. Many tech companies model this same behavior, because Steve Jobs and Apple were hugely successful. However, Jobs represented a risky model, one in which individual charisma holds the team together and not the shared values and goals of the team.

One of my goals in writing this book is to provide you with the tools for creating teams of genius that last beyond your leadership. The leadership tools described in these pages can help you to innovate over the long run, and your team will function well even after you leave.

After you offer data and analysis to your team without being asked, listen to their input. Then permit your team's input to shape the decision in real time. In this way, a genius is part of framing the question the decision addresses.

I want to suggest an even deeper transparency than proactively providing data and obtaining input from a genius before a decision is made. I suggest that you let the genius in on framing the problem itself. Leaders too often make decisions that do not address the key problems they face. A genius can help define whether the decision is even applicable to the problem.

Being transparent means you willingly give up some control of your company. It's a bold and courageous move. Being transparent requires balance for a leader of genius. It is risky and tricky—risky because it makes you vulnerable and tricky because you cannot always predict what information is relevant to a decision. If you pick the wrong information, you may look as if you are withholding something important. If you flood your team with data, the volume can bury what is important.

If you have a hidden agenda or a double standard, a genius will expose it. When you hide the true rationale for a decision from a genius, you are implying that you know better than the genius. You imply that he has nothing to contribute to your reasoning process, or perhaps he would not understand it. This environment will only heighten distrust between you and a genius and decrease creativity.

Rewards of Transparency

Transparency requires work from a leader. It can be time consuming to explain why you are going in a certain direction, but it is worth doing. There are three tangible rewards for being transparent:

1. Transparency builds team unity.
2. Transparency protects you from mistakes.
3. Transparency helps solve problems.

Let's take a closer look at these rewards, and break them down into components.

Transparency builds team unity. A lack of transparency puts a leader at risk of alienating the team. Teams are more productive when the leader discloses not only the data for a decision, but also the rationale for the decision.

One leadership study from the University of Pittsburgh measured charitable contributions in a fund-raising team.[7] The researchers asked the participants if they wanted to know the leader's contributions before making their own. They found that 99 percent of the team wanted the information up front, before they made a commitment. The study also found that when followers had that information, their own contributions increased.

When you hide something from a genius, you treat him like a child, not as someone who is part of the team. By hiding decisions, you imply that the genius has nothing to contribute to your reasoning process or perhaps he would not understand it. Devaluing the intelligence of geniuses is a surefire way to alienate them, because generally the one thing geniuses are certain about is their intelligence. Asking for input on how to frame a decision validates and recognizes the intelligence of a genius by treating her as a peer who is to be reasoned with and convinced.

Transparency builds trust in the leader. When you ask for input on decisions, even if they are unpopular decisions, the genius owns the decision with you. You will be less lonely in a complex and fraught decision-making process.

A specific decision may hurt one department, but be good for the organization as a whole. Providing data beforehand and asking for other methods to achieve the same goal makes the team part of the process of the decision. The employees share in the pain of the department about to have their resources cut.

Ideally, the department that faces losing resources may feel less bitterness, because they were part of the process that searched for alternatives. The equity of the process means that they may be the department that gains next time. This type of decision making demonstrates that you are a thoughtful person and avoids the appearance that your management is random.

Transparency removes speculation and gossip from the dynamics of the team. With a transparent environment, everyone can be much more objective about the direction of the team. They can weigh pros and cons for themselves, and duplicate your thought process individually. If the team arrives at the same conclusions, their trust in you is enhanced. The team might come up with an innovative alternative that is superior to the model you proposed to solve the problem.

Transparency is especially important in stressful situations. If you can explain the relevant information for a decision and get the proper input before it is made, everyone will be moving in the same direction. As mentioned in the last chapter, the team will own the decision and will be more likely to stay cohesive in the face of adversity.

Transparency is a powerful unifier, because everyone loses the right to be offended. You cannot have true transparency without carefully weighing the strengths and weaknesses of every idea and every team member's abilities. You cannot be offended when the team's input is that your proposed solution is inferior, and team members cannot take offense when the consensus solution reassigns their resources or people, because everyone had an equal chance to convince the others.

Proactive transparency increases efficiency. Retroactive transparency can increase the time needed to make and implement a decision, because the leader ends up backtracking to bring others into the loop, starting the decision process over. That is not the case with the proactive transparency I recommend. By bringing geniuses into the process at the beginning, you can objectively match the strengths of the members of your team to the problem being addressed, which will increase the efficiency at which problems are resolved.

This may mean saying difficult things that might be tough for some to swallow. Still, honesty does not mean rudeness, and hard things can be said with courtesy and respect. True transparency means that the team and its leader become vulnerable to each other.

Transparency can protect you from your own stupidity. When you provide the rationale for a decision, you allow others to check your reasoning process and point out errors. Having others evaluate your data can prevent mistakes caused by your subconscious bias.

Getting to Transparent

Besides being more work for you and making you vulnerable to misuse of the shared information, other issues make transparency difficult. Your employees may be unable or unwilling to take part in honest and open communication. This is especially true when you have replaced a beloved leader. The team will compare you to their previous boss, and probably find you wanting, if only from a sense of nostalgia. In this situation, the best method of transition is to start with a transparent bilateral commitment to an organizational philosophy. Shared values are the foundation of team cohesion.

Alternatively, the team may be unable to challenge their own assumptions and self-assess properly. In that case, more information does not help the team get better. Their original assumptions remain unchanged. They may like each other too much or do not know how to disagree without a major argument.

The transition of a team from hoarding information to a culture of transparency starts with you as the leader. You have to start sharing data and its interpretation, welcome challenges, and admit your own mistakes. If you routinely tell the truth and keep it simple, you will not have to change your story for everyone you meet. Each of us has a tendency to make ourselves look better in any information sharing. We also tend to tell the other person what he wants to hear.

Defining the level of transparency each person needs for maximal productivity can be difficult. Deciding with whom to be transparent can be an issue. You could be sharing data and interpretation with the wrong people. If transparency casts a wide net, people whom a decision affects will self-select. You can trust that those people will step forward when they see the relevant information, simply out of self-interest.

You also have to be open to hearing unpleasant information and meet it with calm cheerfulness. Do not kill the messenger. You have to reward or at least approve of contrarian thinking. The broader the range of viewpoints you obtain, the more likely you are to find the correct one. Being transparent with a number of people will help build a culture in which thinking differently is not punished but applauded. This frees genius to be more creative, which is the theme of much of this book.

Proactive candor is contagious. You can build transparency into the fabric of your team. Admitting to an error in your analysis in favor of another opinion will promote growth in the creative freedom of your team. Such behavior can even disarm your critics. You can contain a mistake by admitting you own it. You set boundaries on the mistake by transparently assessing how you made the bad decision in front of your team.

As mentioned, last year I surveyed medical school department chairs across the United States about whether confidence in their leader increased when that person admitted a mistake publicly. A stunning 77 percent said such a disclosure markedly increased their confidence in their leader.

Several years ago, we entered into a relationship with an outlying hospital to provide specialty care. After three years, we were losing a great deal of money and were not able to sustain the effort. At an executive committee meeting, I led a public dissection of what went wrong.

We discovered that we had made many mistaken assumptions. We assumed the demographic data the other hospital gave us was correct, instead of obtaining our own. We assumed that a specific group controlled referral patterns when they did not. That group had promised to support us. They did support us, but they did not have many referrals to begin with. In addition, we were not aware of a competing initiative by another group.

By far, the most important aspect of that initiative was the analysis that took place after it failed. By standing up and leading a discussion of how I made faulty assumptions, my team learned bilateral transparency. They learned they could be creative without fear of retribution for failure. We all shared in both triumphs and failures, and we all ruthlessly and ritually self-assessed together.

Efforts at transparency should be codified into your team's process. Set up regular communication with different clients and end users, consultants, and even competitors to understand the perception of others. Mandate open door hours for all leaders and start blogs on which anyone can make suggestions or register critiques. Establish formal ethics training for everyone, and lead the way yourself.

Making transparency habitual is challenging. If you formalize openness in the organizational structure of your group and schedule it as part of every workflow, transparency will be embedded in the subconscious of the team of genius. When that happens, the team can transcend personality and become productive with interchangeable personnel and different leaders, which creates a team built to last.

Self-Reinforcing Transparency

A team built to last has a repeating and self-reinforcing cycle of transparency. The more you do it, the more insightful and powerful the process of turning over the rocks becomes. Figure 6.1 (next page) demonstrates how this can become a circle.

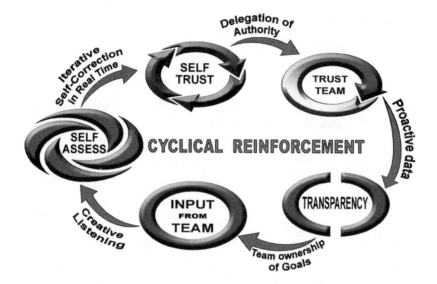

When leaders have confidence in who they are after assessing themselves, they trust their team more easily and delegate authority. The transfer of authority for the project depends on transparency. When your team feels that they have authority over the project, they will own its goals. When they own the project's goals, they will provide the valuable input on the problems facing the project, because they care about its success. They identify with the project, and the completion of the project will be fulfilling.

This transparency comes full circle when the implemented solutions are ruthlessly assessed at a team and individual level. When the team has input on the goals of the project that can change the team's direction, the team becomes a self-reinforcing circle that cannot be broken.

Transparency can initially make you feel more vulnerable, because the information you share decreases the power differential between you and the genius. What you know about organizational plans, resources, and personnel are part of the value you add to genius. Giving that away is a transfer of power to the genius, which can free him to be creative. Ultimately, transparency makes you a stronger leader.

Of course, a genius can make mistakes, for which you will be responsible. I have found that the potential for breakthroughs far outweighs the risk. Leaders of genius who understand that their strength derives from how well geniuses can function will make proactive and bilateral transparency a fundamental principle.

CRUCIAL TAKE-AWAY:

The strength of leaders is measured by how transparent they are before they make a decision.

RULE 5:
ALCHEMY OUTPERFORMS CHEMISTRY

7

To make a major advance today, multiple brilliant people have to work together, each making an important contribution. The way team members interact is crucial to productivity. Technology has become so complicated that the lone genius makes few major advances. By nature individualistic, geniuses are used to thinking differently from others.

Getting a genius to work in a team is difficult. If you force geniuses to be part of a team against their will, you may place constraints on their creativity that can make the team less than the sum of its parts. Instead of the team supporting the genius, the team can restrict the innovation of the genius, and the team will be less productive.

The key to building teams that include geniuses is to use alchemy. Mix a genius with others using nonlinear methods to create unpredictable, even chaotic interactions. I call this type of team building "alchemy," because, like turning lead into gold, the output can be far greater than the input. The output may be much worse or far better than the total intellectual talent on the team. The proper mixing of geniuses is the crucible for creative advances.

The Battle of Giants: Veblen versus Einstein

Flexner created a flow of enormous talent visiting the IAS to interact with the faculty already there and to review their work. These consulting scientists included the Nobel laureates Niels Bohr, John von Neumann, and Paul Dirac. Von Neumann and Dirac had such stimulating experiences while visiting that they later joined the IAS permanently.

However, Flexner failed to understand that the alchemy of personalities was just as important as the intellect on the teams at the IAS. He thought he could put all these geniuses in one place and they would create magical advances. He never took their personalities into account. For example, Flexner put Einstein in the Department of Mathematics, headed by the forceful Oswald Veblen. Einstein was quiet and unassuming. He was the only faculty member in the department whom Veblen had not handpicked, and Veblen was jealous of Einstein's fame.

Einstein was a physicist, and Veblen was a mathematician. Most mathematicians envied the public acclaim theoretical physics received during the past decade. Veblen wrote to Flexner that Einstein only used mathematics as a "tool." And Einstein once commented that mathematicians "sometimes strike me not as if they wanted to help one formulate something clearly, but instead as if they wanted to show us physicists how much brighter they are than we."[1]

These differences led to squabbles over personnel that decreased the productivity of the team. For example, Einstein had come with a mathematician assistant from Germany, Walther Mayer, to whom Flexner had promised a stipend. In fact, one of the reasons Einstein chose the IAS over the California Institute of Technology was because Flexner offered to support Mayer.

After arriving at the IAS, Mayer fell in with the other mathematicians, who offered him assignments and speaking engagements that pulled him away from his work with Einstein. Veblen ultimately offered him an independent position at IAS, leaving Einstein alone without help.

When Einstein asked for another assistant, Veblen, who controlled the budget of the Department of Mathematics, told him there was no money for the position. Veblen disingenuously contended that since Mayer was employed to assist Einstein, that position was already filled. Years later, when Einstein asked for an extension for the Prague physicist Peter Bergmann with whom he was working, Veblen denied him.

In 1936 Einstein and the Polish mathematician Leopold Infeld were making progress on an equation that would unify gravity and electromagnetic waves, which had eluded Einstein for many years. Veblen would not provide an IAS position for Infeld, who could not return to Poland because of the Nazi threat. Einstein made a dramatic appeal to the faculty during a meeting of the Department of Mathematics: "I told them how good you are, and that we are doing important scientific work together . . . but not one of them helped me."[2]

Casting about for work that would support him and allow him to stay in the United States, Infeld instead wrote a popular history of modern physics, using Einstein as his source. This book, *The Evolution of Physics,* sold well and made Infeld far more money than he would have made at the IAS. But Einstein was again left without scientific assistance because of petty personal politics.

Flexner refused to intervene with either Bergmann or Infeld, and he let Veblen control Einstein's resources. Veblen was distracted by his fixation on Einstein's public persona and Einstein had lost his assistant, so neither was as productive as he could have been.

In the end, we are the real losers. Einstein was never able to solve the unification of gravity and electricity in his lifetime, and such a unified field theory remains unsolved today. No one knows what might have happened if Mayer, Bergmann, or Infeld had been able to continue their work with Einstein without interruption.

Shared Purpose as Team Glue

Making teams of geniuses coherent despite widely varying personalities can be difficult, but a diverse team can be glued together with a shared purpose. Lockheed Skunk Works is a Cold War example of innovative team science. Kelly Johnson, a brilliant but tyrannical aeronautical engineer, gathered everyone needed to build an airplane in one room. He gave them few specifications beyond the core mission of the plane they were to build.

Johnson turned them loose to design any shape they wanted with the stipulation that they all had to do it together. He put the designers next to the metallurgists next to the electricians. He thought their proximity would prevent the designers from planning an aircraft that could not be built or could not be wired.

Johnson was hard on his team, but he protected them fiercely. He kept Air Force visits to a minimum. He prohibited making the team any larger than necessary. He paid premium salaries to keep the team together. In response, they built several iconic aircraft in the decades after World War II, including the F-104 Starfighter and the U-2 and SR-71 spy planes. Building these high-tech aircraft pushed the limits of aeronautical engineering. Despite his brilliance, Johnson could never have done it himself. The tasks required a great team.

Johnson ran Skunk Works at the height of the tensions between the Soviet Union and the United States, so he gave his team the shared vision of not just building airplanes but also protecting the country. Teams are made stronger when they share a common mission. When teams share a common motivation to reach the goal set for them, the team becomes more cohesive. When teams all want the same thing for the same reason, they work more closely together. Work becomes a hobby. Team members talk about work as they would talk about golf in their backyards on Saturday afternoon over a beer.

Once Einstein arrived at the IAS, Flexner never gave him a defined mission. Flexner moved on to other recruitments and forgot about his new recruit. Einstein felt lost and was not sure what he should work on. He quipped at one social gathering that his main purpose at the IAS was to be seen, not to do any actual work. Flexner felt he was in no position to tell Einstein what to work on, but this lack of a mission hurt Einstein's productivity at the IAS.

The mission must be challenging enough to provide a sense of pride when it is achieved, yet still within the realm of the achievable, so the team does not give up hope. Achieving the goal has to provide more than a financial reward; it must have significance. Geniuses want a job with meaning. They want to know that their intelligence will make a difference to the world. They feel validated when other very smart people are just as inspired as they are about the project.

Achieving the mission will pull the team closer to one another, transforming distinct personalities into a team. When a vision becomes reality because a team of geniuses worked together to make it come true, they learn that together they are more than the sum of each person.

Adversity Welds Teams Together

A team does not bond until its members encounter adversity and resolve it together. IBM essentially invented the personal computer, but failed to realize that the revenue was in the software, not the hardware. The hardware could be cheaply duplicated. Multiple companies started to sell personal computers that were much less expensive than IBM's. The company lost $8 billion in 1993, the largest single corporate loss in history up to that time. For the first time, they were forced to lay off thousands of workers.

Led by Louis Gerstner, Jr., and later Sam Palmisano, IBM reinvented itself as a provider of high technology services. It got out of the personal computer business completely with the sale of that unit to Lenovo in 2003. IBM bought PriceWaterhouseCooper, the accounting firm, and earned a contract for the U.S. government for cloud computing and data storage. They bought more than two hundred small companies in the IT service provider sector and became the largest provider of servers in the world. Because of IBM's unity of purpose and corporate identity, it came out of that crisis even stronger than before.

The Hewlett Packard Company, commonly known as HP, was going through an identical decision process at the same time. It bickered vociferously about whether it should get out of personal computers, given the abundance of low-priced competitors. Unlike IBM, HP doubled down on PCs and bought Compaq about the same time that IBM sold its PC unit. This was the wrong decision. Currently, HP's net worth is a quarter of IBM's.

IBM and HP faced the same adverse environment. Adversity pushed IBM to pull together, be creative, and come up with risky, innovative solutions. HP hunkered down and tried harder to do what they had always done. Both survived, but only one thrived.

The difference between the HP and IBM teams was the willingness to take risks. IBM was willing to risk the company's survival, HP was not. Because IBM risked everything, there were no boundaries on what it could do. By continuing to pursue what worked in the past, HP limited what it was willing to attempt to overcome the adversity it faced.

IBM took ownership of the situation. Gerstner and Palmisano articulated that IBM had moved too slowly and had failed to recognize that the business was changing. By taking ownership of the problem, it began the process of doing what was necessary to solve it.

Common Misconceptions About Teams

What we commonly believe about teams is not the way successful teams really function. We blindly accept certain ideas about teams without discovering for ourselves what makes a team cohesive and productive. Our misconceptions include:

MYTH #1: A happy team is more productive than a grumpy team. We believe this, because it is easier to lead a happy team. J. Richard Hackman at Harvard University conducted a study on symphonies and discovered this belief was not true.[3] The study found that peevish musicians played together slightly better than happy orchestras. The researchers concluded that the mood before and during a task does not predict excellence. What is most important is the mood after a task is completed. A team performs best when it is slightly uncomfortable and stretched beyond what its members think they can do, when they have to rise to a challenge. When team members feel satisfied before a task, they tend to perform worse.

MYTH #2: The bigger the team, the better it performs. Most leaders feel that the larger the team is, the more accomplished. Behind this belief, we like to lead larger teams, because it feeds our perception of importance. Leading a large team makes us feel superior to someone leading a small team.

The Harvard study found that as a team gets bigger the links needed for it to function rise exponentially. Ultimately, the sheer weight of communicating to everyone becomes unwieldy, and the team collapses. Hackman's upper limit for team size is nine.

MYTH #3: Teams need to be refreshed periodically with an influx of new talent to keep from getting stale. On the contrary, teams that know each other well perform better. This is not to say that you should never bring in new expertise. The point is not to reorganize a team just for the sake of newness and innovation, which will only generate more mistakes.

The National Transportation Safety Board reported that 73 percent of accidents happened on a crew's first day of flying together. In addition, a NASA study discovered that even fatigued crews with a history of working together made half as many errors as crews of rested pilots who had never flown together.

The Strategic Air Command (SAC) supervises the Air Force planes carrying nuclear weapons. SAC teams performed better than any other flight crews studied. They trained together as a crew, and they became superb at working together because they had to.

When you are working together in real time and there can be no mistakes, you want to keep your teams together for years, rather than constantly changing their composition. SAC never made a major mistake during the Cold War, as evidenced by the fact we are still here, and not a radioactive crisp in a nuclear desert.

MYTH #4: A strong team leader is essential. Most leaders want to project strength and confidence to improve team cohesion and motivation. This is fine with most team members, but not with geniuses. A genius will rebel against coercive leadership, and the productivity of the team will be diminished.

Ways to Kill a Team

Teams are living organisms. They need to be fed and watered. They can be killed. A leader's toxic behavior can destroy a team in two major ways:

1. Playing Favorites

If your employees perceive that you prefer one team member over others, the ill-favored employees will get discouraged and be less productive. Cliques will form around each pole, the favorite and her fans versus the disgruntled majority, who will unite around the unfairness of their position.

Even the perception that favoritism is happening will cripple a team. Dr. Mike Good, dean at the University of Florida College of Medicine and inventor of the computerized patient simulator, said, "My departments are like my children, and I love all my children equally."

The quality of innovation depends on whether leadership gives preferential treatment to specific people who do not merit it, according to Alina Mungiu-Pippidi at the Hertie School of Government in Germany.[4] She studied research, development, and new intellectual property in countries in which the majority of government contracts are given to a single bidder.

The single bidders often had a personal or financial relationship with someone in the government. She found that the innovation in these countries lagged far behind the countries that award contracts based only on quality and cost. The study showed that favoritism destroys innovation. Geniuses flee to meritocratic countries or become unproductive. The same is true of organizations in the United States.

2. Not Delegating Authority with Responsibility

Delegating is crucial to team building, because it shows that you trust the team. The team knows you believe in them when you delegate essential steps toward the goal.

You hire genius because they know how to do things that you do not. Unless you delegate properly, you are wasting genius. If you do not delegate tasks appropriately, you may find yourself too busy to meet with the team. You become unapproachable and can miss great opportunities for technological advancement, because people will not walk in with their innovative ideas.

What you delegate is important. The team's goal must not be sliced too thin or too thick. Tasks need to be at the intersection of what the team needs done, the individual's training, and what the individual enjoys doing. What geniuses enjoy doing may not be what they were trained to do or what the team needs them to do. The job of a leader is to find that intersection.

Nonlinear Teams

The most productive teams are nonlinear. By that I mean that the output is not proportional to or predictable from the input. This can work both ways. A team of several geniuses can spend a fortune and do nothing just as easily as they can come up with a way to incorporate quantum computing into laptops. The point of leading genius is to achieve a transformative breakthrough, an unforeseen leap in your field. To do this, teams must have an element of unpredictability.

Marcial Losada, a Chilean psychologist, applied nonlinear dynamics, a form of mathematical analysis to measure the changing interactions of business teams.[5] Teams with low performance were locked in advocacy and self-orientation and tended to have very controlled environments. These low-performing teams lost the chaos that generates the best creativity. When the interactions revolved around just a few members, the team became predictable.

On failing teams, communication was dominated by a few members with charismatic personalities, not necessarily the best ideas. Team members who dominated the interactions became poles around which all work converged and all communication resonated. New problems were met with old solutions, and progress stalled. The poles become stronger over time, and the communication patterns become cemented the more they were used.

Losada found that each member on the best performing teams interacted with an average of four other members, and these interactions were unpredictable and constantly changing.

Einstein loved unpredictable interactions. One of the best-known examples is his long walks with Kurt Gödel, a younger mathematician at the IAS. During this time, Gödel published proofs on logic that provided the foundation for computer science. He later acknowledged that his talks with Einstein were transformative. Einstein's thought process was not parallel with Gödel's, and this led Gödel into new territory.

Building a Nonlinear Team

A team of geniuses does not automatically make a genius team. Teams are not the sum of their parts. Achievements are not correlated with the average intelligence of the group. In addition, creativity is not correlated with the maximum intelligence of any given individual in the group. Only with a nonlinear team can you achieve a transformative advance.

To create teams for which nonlinear interactions are habitual, leaders cannot define interactions, either intentionally or unintentionally. Instead, they should mandate a continuously shifting leadership of the discussion, giving alternating opinions equal voice. Each team member has to feel safe to offer his thoughts.

The team must have a flat hierarchy, which means the leader is not seen above other team members. Little distance in power and in communication exists between the leader and the team members. A group's intellectual achievements are correlated with the equality of taking turns in a conversation and the proportion of women on the team.[6] Women are better at allowing others to speak, and this will lead to more innovation and creativity.

Figure 7.1 depicts the power of teams with flattened hierarchies and nonlinear communication. Linear communication, shown on the left, is hierarchical, like the military. The leader tells a few subordinates, who in turn tell the next level. With a linear team structure, the message can be changed from level to level, either on purpose or by mistake. This is slower than communicating in a team with a flat hierarchy, in which everyone hears the same communication at the same time.

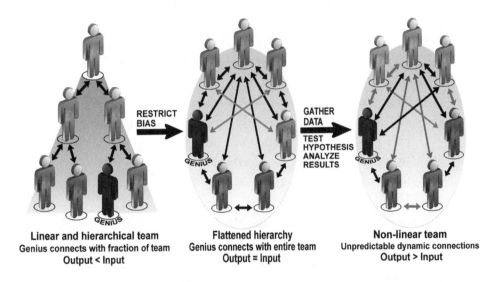

Linear and hierarchical team	Flattened hierarchy	Non-linear team
Genius connects with fraction of team	Genius connects with entire team	Unpredictable dynamic connections
Output < Input	Output = Input	Output > Input

A flattened hierarchy means that there are fewer barriers to feedback from the team on any given communication. Nonlinear teams can only form in flat hierarchies, when the leader diffuses her authority among the team members. Team members take turns leading the discussion in an unpredictable manner, not just depending on their expertise, nor on their personality. Instead, the leader of a discussion is a person who has an innovative idea. Nonlinear discussions can only occur when there is mutual respect among team members, each believing any one of his colleagues could have something valuable to contribute.

A Team That Looks Like You Will Fail

The easiest team to manage is one that looks like you, in which everyone thinks like you and works on your schedule. You will resonate with this team, and you will have the most fun working with people like you. You will probably be inclined to spend time outside of work with this team. But this team will most likely fail at the project. The team will have all of your strengths and all of your weaknesses.

A team composed of people like you will lack nonlinear interactions among team members with unique skills. Such a team will have poles around which all interactions resonate, which will set boundaries on creativity and limit innovative approaches to problems. If a team is like you, it will have only one approach to problems, only one process for workflow, only one way to communicate, and only the perseverance you have yourself.

To build a successful team, you have to self-assess accurately what skills and experience you lack and which personalities differ from you (Rule 1). To pay full attention, you have to be genuinely curious about what anyone on your team says. That curiosity allows you to be patient and lets a nonlinear dynamic unfold for your team. It allows you to creatively listen (Rule 3).

You need to build a team that is the anti-you. Whoever is not like you is a candidate for your team. Be careful about choosing close friends for the team, unless they are fearless about staking out their own positions and defending themselves against you. Close friends often end up acting and thinking like each other, which can make a team look like you after all.

The Team as an End in Itself

A giddy dance happens when a team bounces ideas back and forth, arguing, cursing, and laughing. The bizarre is discussed as normal, and normal is seen in the rear-view mirror. You will look back at these meetings with fondness, because at one of those meetings your team will have an insight that will change your field forever. When this happens, the team becomes an end in itself, and members work for the team more than the paycheck.

Building teams may be the hardest thing to do in leading geniuses. You cannot be afraid of correcting the course. You must not fear risk or disciplining people smarter than you. You have to manage both an aggressive genius and a shy genius in unique ways. You have to be able to change approaches at a moment's notice, because technological advances do not take place on your schedule. You have to tailor incentives based on individuals, yet you have to keep the team sharing a single vision.

You need a gentle hand in leading teams of genius. Forcing a team to a different goal can be destructive. The tactic will automatically result in pushback from genius, especially if your decision is not data-driven. When members of the team all buy into different goals at different rates, the team can become disjointed with some motivated to work toward the new goal and others not.

Having a nonlinear team does not mean total chaos, with everyone doing what she or he wants. The work of the leader is to keep the team focused on the shared goal while letting them wander freely over all possible mechanisms to achieve that goal.

Building teams that last is an art as well as a science, alchemy as well as chemistry. We talked earlier about the mathematics behind successful teams, but there is a subconscious emotional intelligence to the effort as well. Understanding the hopes and fears of each member of the team takes a great deal of effort, but it increases the potential for transformative interactions.

The best teams are more than professional organizations. They are living organisms that adapt and grow as the environment changes. They connect through mutual respect for each other's talents, which enables each team member to listen and take ideas and arguments from every other member. The best teams can be extraordinarily creative and can solve problems that would otherwise be impossible barriers, because together the team stretches beyond normal boundaries.

More than two decades ago, I worked with a general practice physician and an ophthalmologist, in the same clinic at Indiana University Medical Center. The ophthalmologist spent a summer in Saint Petersburg, Russia working in a free clinic on a medical outreach trip.

An eighteen-year-old boy came to him with a bulging eyeball. My friend found that the reason for the bulging was because the boy had a Hodgkin's lymphoma growing behind his eye. Hodgkin's lymphoma in the United States is a curable cancer, but it was a death sentence in Russia if the patient was poor.

The ophthalmologist had no way to give intravenous chemotherapy in his clinic. He called us and asked if there was anything that could be done. I put together a chemotherapy regimen of pills that could be taken by mouth, yet still be curative. I purchased all the drugs myself and packaged them up carefully. A Russian professor at the university translated the instructions, and my general practitioner friend traveled to Russia to hand-deliver the box to the ophthalmologist, because the mail was not trustworthy in Russia.

The ophthalmologist gave the boy his first and second doses of chemotherapy before returning to the United States. He was able to see the young man achieve a complete remission. He taught the boy's mother to administer the remaining chemotherapy. We were an organic nonlinear team at its best, solving an untraditional problem through an innovative mechanism.

CRUCIAL TAKE-AWAY

Psychological cohesion can spark as many creative combustions as intellectual expertise.

RULE 6:
YOUR PAST IS NOT THE FUTURE'S TRUTH

8

HiPPOs control every meeting. According to Avinash Kaushik, CEO of Market Motive, who created the acronym, they trample analyses and push aside every strategy.[1] HiPPOs throw their weight around without even realizing it, blind to the havoc they wreak. They stifle creative discussion.

HiPPOs are the "Highest Paid Person's Opinions." The size of their salary automatically gives their opinion greater weight than any data. Their opinion is treated as fact, as if it came from careful analysis of gigabytes of relevant data. Many leaders pontificate on complex issues based on their past experience without taking the time to analyze the underlying complexities. They use anecdotes to make billion dollar decisions.

One anecdote should not be data, and two anecdotes should not generate a policy, yet many organizations are run on the experience of one or two people. Even if those people are smart and hardworking, they can never match the systematic gathering and analysis of data on any question. Leaders fall into the trap of making decisions based on their past experiences all the time.

Never lead a genius using your past experience to make decisions. She or he will immediately recognize when your opinion is driving the decision, and you will lose credibility. Your instinct and your experience work well for putting teams together, and in choosing whom to trust. Data are more important when you are making a decision on a strategic goal or a tactical process to reach that goal.

"We as leaders are all anchored to our last bad experience," says Dr. Tim Flynn, former chair of the Accreditation Council for Graduate Medical Education. Though we might deny it, we use our own experiences much more often than we use relevant data to make decisions, simply because it is already ours.

Flexner Knew His Own Ignorance

Flexner initially understood when he did not have the knowledge to make crucial decisions, and he worked hard to obtain relevant data. For example, when the Carnegie Foundation asked Flexner to put together a report on the state of medical education in the United States and Europe in 1908, he recognized that he knew nothing about medical schools. He began by gathering as much data as possible.

Instead of relying on secondhand sources, he personally visited all 155 medical schools in the United States and many in Europe as well. He sat through classes and interviewed many students and faculty. He worked hard to obtain as much data as possible. While visiting the University of Iowa College of Medicine, the dean told him that the classrooms were locked and the janitor with the key was out for the day. Flexner let the dean take him to the train station where they said goodbye, but he sensed the dean's deception. Flexner immediately caught a ride back to the medical school, found the janitor to open the classrooms, and saw that most were empty of the equipment needed to teach medical students. The dean's attempt to cover up failed completely because Flexner wanted evidence and not opinion.

When Flexner started his data gathering, local physicians privately owned most medical schools, from which they made a profit by charging tuition. There were few full-time faculty, most schools only required a high school education, and there were no limits to admissions. Access to laboratories or to hospitals for training in physical exams and diagnosis was nonexistent.

Not known for tact, Flexner pulled no punches. His report on medical education was notorious for its harsh description of many medical schools. For example, he said that California Medical College "is a disgrace to the state whose laws permit its existence."[2] He had firsthand data on these medical schools, and no one challenged him because of that. He realized that to change an entire nation's medical educational process he would have to be convincing. He could only do that with a mountain of factual evidence.

Flexner's study had great influence on medical education. In the next twenty-five years, more than half of U.S. medical schools closed, including all the proprietary for-profit schools. Medical schools made their admission requirements much more stringent, and the vast majority became associated with a university to improve their academic standing.

Flexner also refused to let the past dictate the future with his groundbreaking hiring of women and Jewish immigrants as faculty at the IAS. Most major American universities had unwritten quotas for Jewish students and Jewish faculty, despite their qualifications. Flexner broke with the past and hired many Jewish scientists at the IAS.

The success of the IAS led to competition among major universities for the brightest scientists, regardless of their ethnicity. Flexner did more to change the prejudice that affected the hiring of scientists than any other figure or cultural intervention.

In addition, women faculty at major scientific institutions were extremely rare. Flexner thought that such bias was responsible for a waste of talent. "In the appointments to the staff and faculty as well as in the admission of workers and students, no account shall be taken, directly or indirectly, of race, religion, or sex," he wrote at the founding of the IAS.[3] Years later, when funds became tighter during the lingering Depression, he failed to fulfill his promise to pay the women faculty equally with the men.

Flexner Had His Own Biases

Flexner should rightly be considered a hero for hiring women faculty. He hired Hetty Goldman to a tenured IAS position when tenured faculty positions for women were uncommon. Despite opposition from other major universities, he made the groundbreaking move. However, he thought that employment alone was sufficient to earn Hetty Goldman's gratitude, though he paid her much less than her male colleagues. He kept promising to adjust her salary to be equitable, but he never did. When she complained that he had not kept his promise, he could not understand why she was not grateful just to have a faculty job, displaying an undeniable gender bias.

Flexner had an unconscious racial bias, common for that time. As mentioned, he proposed closing five of the seven black medical schools. He thought that black physicians should only treat patients of the same race and should be supervised by white physicians. He went on to advance the idea that African Americans were a health threat to Caucasians, because they spread tuberculosis. This discrimination decreased African American access to health care for several generations.

Gut Instincts

Many believe that rapid decisions using experience-based intuition are more accurate than decisions arrived at through slow and careful analysis of the data. There is evidence that intuition may work with interpersonal judgments, for example, evaluating if a person is trustworthy. Since everyone has a lot of experience interacting with liars and truth-tellers, experience could support such evaluations. This might work for normal decisions, but it does not work well for teams of genius. Leadership would be much easier if it did.

Experience is a poor teacher in science and technology, because advances come from doing what has not been done before. Past experience rarely can guide technological research decisions. Despite protests to the contrary, many business leaders still make most of their decisions based on emotion. They justify the decisions rationally later. A study by the Fortune Knowledge Group found that 62 percent of business leaders relied on gut feelings to make decisions.[4] A report in The Economist Intelligence Unit (EIU) cited by *CIO* digital magazine found that 73 percent of surveyed business leaders trusted their own intuition to make decisions, and 68 percent said that they trusted their instincts over data.[5]

Leading by intuition based on past experience is so much easier because analyzing data can be so tedious.

Mistrusting Your Gut

Organizations make colossal mistakes because they trust the instinct of their leaders. Since most leaders bury their poor decisions, we do not hear about most of the mistakes. One of the most famous instinct-driven decisions in modern business was Time Warner's purchase of AOL. Time Warner CEO Jerry Levin forced the deal past his reluctant board. There were carefully marshalled, data-driven arguments on one side against the purchase, and there was Levin on the other. Levin prevailed, because he was the HiPPO. A few years later, Levin admitted that the forced merger was one of the worst business deals of the century. He eventually resigned as CEO. Time Warner took a $99 billion loss only two years after the purchase.

Even Einstein was misled by his gut. Though his theory of relativity led to the invention of quantum mechanics, Einstein instinctively mistrusted quantum mechanics, which holds that an electron can be in two places at once. Einstein disliked that indeterminacy immensely. He called quantum mechanics, "Spooky actions at a distance."[6]

He vigorously debated with Niels Bohr on the subject. Einstein took the position that physicists used quantum mechanics because they had not yet discovered the hidden variables that would allow them to calculate the exact single location of atomic particles. Robert Oppenheimer, who became director of the IAS after completing the Manhattan Project, said that Einstein instinctively did not like the "abandonment of continuity or causality."[7]

Einstein was wrong. His instinct was that God "is not playing at dice" with the universe, as he famously said later.[8] Einstein's distrust of this new way of thinking about reality was odd. After all, he had led the previous revolution in how we perceive the universe. Einstein had put "the dagger in the hand of the assassin of his own work," Oppenheimer wrote. "He fought with the theory he fathered, but which he hated. It was not the first time that this has happened in science."[9]

Einstein's distrust of quantum mechanics limited his productivity in the latter part of his career at the IAS. If Einstein can be boxed in by his instinct, this trap is even more fraught with risk for us non-geniuses.

We are imprisoned by our own personal biases to which we are often blind. A careful analysis of complete data will not persuade us. We are quick to trust our instincts despite the multitude of data showing our judgment is off.

Blinding Ourselves

Einstein himself faced intense opposition to his theory of relativity from German physicists solely because he was Jewish. Rudolf Tomaschek, the director of the Institute of Physics at Dresden, wrote: "Modern physics is an instrument of Jewry for the destruction of Nordic science. True physics is the creation of the German spirit."[10]

Perhaps Einstein's most combative opponent was Philipp Lenard, who wrote that science was not international, but "like every other human product is racial and conditioned by blood."[11]

Tomaschek and Lenard let their preconceived ideas about race blind them to the greatest advance in physics in their generation. By allowing their prejudice to blind them, they set German physics back decades. They are arguably the reason Germany lost World War II, because they refused to accept the principles that would have allowed Germany to develop the first atomic weapon. The philosophical foundations of the Nazi empire led to their losing the war, because the Nazis bent physical truth for political aims.

The blind spots of Lenard and Tomaschek seem obvious, but recognizing our own blind spots is difficult, which is why we need the wisdom of crowds, not just crowds of data, but crowds of people. Other people serve as checks and balances for our own biases, but we have to listen to them, as in Rule 3. You should formalize a process by which you analyze the analysis of the data itself. Similar to Rule 1, you need to not only make sure you gather the right data, but that you are ruthlessly unbiased in its analysis.

Biases That Shape Decisions

There is solid research on how cognitive biases affect decision making, which demonstrates that gut feelings are not to be trusted. To make data-driven decisions, you have to realize that you often make emotion-driven decisions that are biased in ways you do not even realize. Biases that you do not recognize but that drive your decision making are called *implicit biases*.

There has been a subtle but fundamental shift in our culture that makes data-driven leadership more difficult. What seems to matter now are not facts, but certainty. If I am more certain about a decision than you are, then I win, no matter what the facts are. The more certain people are about a decision, the more persuasively they can communicate. Their passion for their position can overwhelm the facts. Certainty can come from multiple types of bias, listed below, that are implicit, beneath our consciousness.

Centrality Bias

Centrality bias is a common, fundamental bias that shapes our decision-making process. With centrality bias, we believe that if the data were important, we would already know it. We mistrust new information, because it did not come from us. In the EIU study, only 54 percent of executives queried said they would reanalyze the data if it did not agree with their intuition. This is irrational.

We have centrality bias, because we exist as a unit of self, as one person. What is most important about work is not to make money but to maintain our sense of identity. This is why self-assessment is so difficult. It means regularly breaking your identity down and rebuilding it into one closer to reality.

Many leaders live on a gambler's high, addicted to making decisions based on their instinct, because they get the same adrenaline rush as a blackjack player. These leaders justify this behavior by assuming they alone have the special knowledge to make this decision. Their brains need fear-induced adrenaline to feel normal.

Self-Serving Bias

Self-serving bias causes us to dismiss facts and processes if they threaten our self-esteem and our sense of accomplishment. This type of bias makes us give more weight to facts that validate our past choices. We are driven to take credit for success even when we were dragged against our will in that direction.

Today, we tend to trust individual experts over systematically collected data that has been mathematically analyzed, but this does not work in an environment that is rapidly changing. We fail to match the solution to the problem, because the problem is different than any before it. Our past patterns of failure and success can trick us into thinking our current project is structurally similar. These past patterns heavily influence our intuition.

Basing decisions on past experience and instinct is often an exercise in power. Do it this way, because *I* want it done this way. Many leaders take credit when they make the right choice by intuition and deflect blame when they make a mistake.

To make data-driven versus instinctual decisions, you have to let go of the drive for individual power that your self-esteem is built upon and dissolve your leadership into a crowd. The more a leader mistrusts himself, the more he is likely to want to maintain individual decision-making power.

Anchoring Bias

We can become irrationally certain about a decision by giving more importance to the information we received first. Anchoring bias prompts us to form early decision trees with the initial data we hear. Almost no one can wait until all the data has been analyzed before categorizing it. Waiting for all the data before making a decision would have been an evolutionary disadvantage. For example, early humans learned not to wait to see if a predator at the waterhole was hungry or not.

Status Quo Bias

People feel more pain at loss than joy at gain. This tendency results in the status quo bias. We uphold established approaches in the face of new obstacles, because we fear that change will result in loss. We are inclined to give more weight to data that reinforces the status quo. We are skeptical about any analysis of the data that suggests a change of perception or a change of course, because we fear loss.

You often uphold the status quo without even realizing it. You think you are leading change when all you have done is rearrange the furniture. To assess whether you are operating with the status quo bias, try a thought experiment known as the Reversal Test. Analyze the risks and benefits of doing the opposite of the status quo. If change is the better choice, then doing the opposite of the status quo should have fewer costs and greater rewards. In that case, changing direction is the right decision.

When closing a major merger or acquisition, Warren Buffet hires two groups of attorneys. He pays them both a base rate, but he pays one group more if the deal goes through, and the other more if the deal fails. That is how he builds the Reversal Test into his process.

Belief Bias

Belief bias is the tendency to judge the strength of an argument on the plausibility of the conclusion. If a conclusion makes sense based on previous experience, we give more weight to the data and analysis leading to that conclusion. This bias involves gathering all relevant data, but then fitting it into our preconceived worldview and using it to make a faith-based decision.

Survivor Bias

As discussed, the temptation to pick and choose the data we analyze can lead to distorted conclusions, which can lead to the survivor bias. More weight is given to the success of one decision if the results of that decision are still around. If that same decision led to failure, we ignore it in the future. We assume that the continued existence of one concept means that it has been tested and found to be helpful and true.

A few years ago, an extremely expensive lung cancer drug, which helped only about 10 percent of patients, was approved by the FDA, because the people helped by the drug showed up at the public hearing and were vociferously supportive. Dr. David Johnson, a lung cancer expert, sadly observed to me that none of the dead patients made it to the hearing. His point was that the drug may have actually hurt the other 90 percent, but they were not around to complain.

Confirmation Bias

Leaders insist on trusting their instinct, regardless of the evidence that data-driven decisions have better outcomes. One reason for this is the sheer amount of data available. In 2014, the Library of Congress web archives were growing at 5 terabytes per month, and that rate has rapidly increased.

The tsunami of data can become overwhelming. You cannot even begin to think about where to start analyzing it. You break it into smaller pieces and choose what to consider. When you do that, you generate blind spots, because you select data according to your past experience. "You can make data say anything you want," Ed Jimenez, CEO of Shands Teaching Hospital, said. "Using it and interpreting it correctly is more complicated."

With confirmation bias, you tend to believe data that confirms what you already think. As you try to analyze the complete set of relevant data, you perceive patterns that confirm what you have seen before or what you currently think. After you gather the relevant data, picking which facts to pay attention to is the first opportunity for distortion. Too often leaders think, "I know the truth; now let's go find facts to back that up."

When you have a personal stake in the outcome of any decision, you will make emotionally biased judgments about what data to consider. Getting around these blind spots is complicated. Doing so takes exceptional intellectual rigor.

Are We Even Asking the Right Questions?

The obvious question to ask in reviewing decisions is the outcome—did the decision reach its predetermined metric of success? Leaders of geniuses can save themselves a great deal of trouble if they assess whether the decision was framed in the proper manner in the first place. You have to consider whether you are asking the right question.

You could be making a decision based on something that is irrelevant to the goals of your team.

For example, in 1999, a Mars Lander crashed, because members of one team did not translate their metric measurements to another team's Imperial measurements. Billions of dollars spent on the project were wasted, because no one decided beforehand which measurement system to use. What the project needed was one manager to worry about the mundane and boring details.

Attention to details is especially important for leading genius, because genius often skips the small stuff. When teaching at the University of California, Robert Oppenheimer would cover the chalkboard with complex quantum mechanics equations. When asked by a timorous student where the equation was that he was referring to, he pointed to an unintelligible scrawl of symbols, and said it was underneath the mass of squiggles. He had written over it with another equation because he thought the first was so obvious.[12]

The work of genius is not obvious to non-geniuses. Equations need to be carefully defined, because if they are not, the team could have a disaster, such as crashing a billion-dollar space probe.

The attitude of "Don't sweat the small stuff" is dangerous in most science and technology fields. The job of a leader of genius is to sweat the details. "It is always what you do not see coming that does the most damage," David Guzick, vice president at the University of Florida has said. This is how you add value to genius. You focus on the details, so nothing takes the team by surprise.

You can contribute by finding gaps in the details of the project and asking questions about those holes. You can serve as the institutional memory of the group by remembering which assumptions worked and which did not. As Colin Powell has said: "Never neglect details. When everyone's mind is dulled or distracted, the leader must be doubly vigilant."[13]

Gathering all the data before making a decision prevents you from repeating a mistake someone else has already made. Einstein used to walk to work with David Mitrany, a political scientist also employed at the IAS. One day he confided to Mitrany that he thought he had finally found the theory unifying gravity and electricity, the long sought Unified Field Theory. Six months later, Einstein off-handedly mentioned that his theory did not work, but he was going to publish it anyway. Surprised, Mitrany asked why. "To save another fool from wasting six months on the same idea," Einstein responded.[14]

The Decision Is Not About You

Creating a data-driven culture for decision making is not magic. You can do it with a few significant shifts in how you and your team think. The first is to depersonalize the decision process. Many leaders assume that the decision is about them in some manner. Even Harry Truman's famous quote on accountability, "The buck stops here," is a trap. Leaders can think they are taking responsibility for a decision, but they are actually making the decision based on how it affects their self-esteem.

A colleague told me about a pharmaceutical executive who could not separate discussion about past decisions from his self-esteem. He became defensive and hostile whenever a consensus agreed that one of his past decisions led to an unproductive path. His face would get red, his voice shrill, and he would attack whoever was speaking.

A decision should rest not on how it affects you or even your team, but on how the direction will help the team to reach goals that have intrinsic worth. The goals must be external to you and to the team. If you quit or the team dissolves, the goals remain unchanged. Keeping the goals external can become tricky, because you need some emotional investment to implement a decision. Emotion should come after you reach the decision, not before. Becoming emotionally invested in a decision will enhance effort and creativity.

Data analysis should use as many benchmarks within and outside the company as possible, which makes the decision much less personal. You should use external reviewers and include internal stakeholders whom the decision may affect. Get contrarian opinions. Pay someone to punch holes in the idea, and do not get offended when they do. The concept of hedge funds is buying a position opposite to their major investment to prevent crippling losses.

Implementing Decisions

This might sound as if we need to become robots, devoid of emotions, but this is not true. The fact is that the way our brains hold on to decisions is based on emotion. Emotion gives us the backbone to stick with the decision we have made. Ever sat across from your board, and despite overwhelming evidence for your proposal, they do not approve it? Nothing you can say persuades them to change their minds. As decision making becomes harder and more complex, emotions are needed to implement the decision. A leader has to recognize the logic of the analyzed data and identify with it on a personal level. A leader has to desire to do what the data suggest is correct.

It takes an emotional commitment to a decision to see it through. Unfortunately, many leaders forget the first step in making a decision: rationally comparing all the available data, before making an emotional commitment. Both are important for solid decision making. If you have rational comparison without emotion, you cannot stick to a decision. With emotive decision making, you can make firm commitments to the wrong direction and will not listen to advice.

Freedom from Bias

We all have implicit biases that will not only contaminate any decision we make but will also taint the gathering of data itself. Unless you self-assess before gathering data, the weight of your bias will pull you into instinctual decisions.

Our brains are hard-wired to make rapid decisions by subconsciously weighing the sum of emotional price tags on similar past experiences. We put an emotional price tag on past events based on how they affected our psychological wellbeing, not whether they actually helped us or the team reach goals. We rationally analyze the risks and benefits of any decision less often than we think. Many times, even when carefully parsing the known data, we have already made a subconscious decision and are only looking for data that confirms our suspicions. Because we do this without realizing it, we need to recognize when we are making these instinctual decisions as we go through the motions of a rational decision.

Before making any final decision, you should go through a five-step process we devised to prevent you from fooling yourself that you are making a rational decision when your instincts and emotions have already decided. For example, say you have a choice between buying a promising yet untested new cancer drug from a small biotech company or developing your own drug. Write down the answers to these five questions and then go over them with your team in a transparent manner to make sure you are not fooling yourself on the answers.

1. **Do I really have all the information needed to make a decision?** We all have an intuition about what will happen in the future. Even trained statisticians think a small sample from the present can be used to predict the future. We use our own experiences as that small sample. This is called the "Belief in the Law of Small Numbers."[15] This is the reason why casinos stay in business. Our brains think we can intuit the future behavior of slot machines or biotech companies based on a small sample of the present. Though there are obvious differences between slot machines and biotech companies, we can make the same mistake with both. In this case, my past experience with new cancer drugs might lead me to overestimate the value of the information I have on the biotech company or on my team's ability. If several other recent drug candidates from

this biotech company have been successful, survivor bias influences me to think that I have all the information needed, but the failures must also be taken into account.

2. **Who benefits and who loses if I buy the biotech company's drug versus developing my own?** In this case, self-serving bias influences me to develop a cancer drug using my own team instead of buying the drug from another company. I would benefit in terms of prestige if my own team developed a successful cancer drug. My team would benefit, because developing a successful cancer drug is an important mission. The biotech company would lose a sale.

3. **What happened the last time I faced a similar situation?** The more recent the loss, the more it influences my decision, which is how anchoring bias works. If a recent similar decision turned out poorly, then loss aversion makes me less likely to go in the same direction. You should not let any single past adverse event overwhelm your strategic goals. Sunk costs are already lost. Your current decision must be independent of all past decisions. This is especially hard if those decisions were your own.

4. **What happens if I do the opposite?** If modeling it results in more gain than the proposed decision, then our data or assumptions are wrong. Examining what happens if the opposite direction is taken can prevent centrality bias. Centrality bias makes me think that the data I already have are more significant to the decision and my ability to make a decision is better than anyone else's. Rule 1 should tell me that I am far less essential to the decision than I think.

5. **How many assumptions have to be made for the best outcome to occur?** The more assumptions I make, the chance of error rises. In the process, we often mistake assumptions for data to support an instinctual decision. If my past experiences confirm a decision I want to make for my own self-esteem or to confirm a worldview I hold, I assume a past experience is data. Belief bias and confirmation bias can make me think that the assumptions I have

made from my past are an accurate prediction of the future. This is self-deception at work.

You must define up front what choices your biases lead you to, and you must be sensitive to your inclination toward these choices. You must avoid gathering data only from sources that would confirm the choice you think is right because of your biases. You must avoid discounting data that appears to be contrary to the choices these biases would promote. See Figure 8.1: Unbiased data gathering is weighed down by your past experiences and your belief systems.

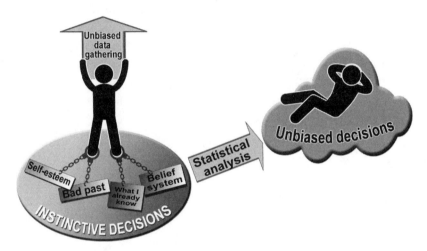

I have sat on executive boards that used data to make important strategic decisions without a statistical analysis of the data. It is not enough to just gather data in an unbiased manner; it also must be statistically analyzed, which is a good way to free yourself from your implicit biases.

How suspicious you are of bias and how carefully you analyze the data should rise in proportion to the cost of the decision, which is not just measured in money, but also in terms of setting precedents and promoting productivity and creativity. Genius will appreciate such careful analysis and will be more likely to accept the decision. You can best support the work of a genius with careful decision making. This process builds the team and enhances its cohesion toward the project's goal.

CRUCIAL TAKE-AWAY

Be continuously suspicious of your instincts.

RULE 7:
IGNORE SQUIRRELS

9

Many geniuses are like Labrador retrievers chasing squirrels. Geniuses cannot stop themselves from chasing the good ideas that flash across their vision at full speed. When another interesting concept comes to their attention, they pivot on a dime, and are off in a new direction, chasing that concept.

Being distracted by interesting ideas is easier and livelier than being focused. The life of the Labrador retriever is full of passion and excitement. It is far more stirring to chase squirrels than to walk quietly at someone's side.

For the leader of genius, the perfect accomplishment is the enemy of the good accomplishment. Chasing the perfect idea may distract the genius from getting anything productive done at all. There will always be a better idea that comes along that will take precedence over the current concept. Chasing squirrels can be a drain on productivity. Having the focus to take a good idea all the way to commercialization takes perseverance, something that a genius does not always have. If a genius leads your team off on a squirrel hunt, the team will never be able to reach their original goal.

Focusing a Vision Makes It Stronger

In 1930, the Bambergers had bought into Flexner's vision of a science institute and gave him control of the IAS, naming him director.

Flexner knew that the IAS could not compete in everything. He wanted to be world class in just a few areas. When he started the IAS, Flexner decided to focus on mathematics. Veblen, Einstein, and Hermann Weyl were his best recruits from that early era, and they were the best in the world. When he concentrated his resources and went after the very best scientists in the world in these chosen areas, he got them. His focused approach was a crucial step to innovation, as advances come at the ends of knowledge. To get past what is already known you have to narrow the vision.

Flexner was committed to the core mission of the IAS as a dedicated oasis of scientific advancement and refused to accept students into the IAS or give degrees like most institutes of higher learning. He maintained this vision despite the occasional protest from some faculty who wanted the IAS to be similar to more traditional universities.

Flexner believed teaching classes would take researchers away from their experiments and that mentoring Ph.D. students would take the faculty's focus off their own work. "The Institute is, from the standpoint of organization, the simplest and least formal thing imaginable," he wrote.[1]

The geniuses at IAS were sequestered in a monastery-like, rural atmosphere where they could focus exclusively on their work. There were few distractions. Noticing the scientists' dedication, the wife of a visiting British scholar asked Flexner, "Does everyone work until 2 o'clock in the morning?"[2]

Narrowing focus makes it denser and stronger, like a nail. I once asked one of my scientists if he was strong enough to take a hammer and pound it through the walnut table we were sitting at.

"Of course not," he answered, "The hammer is too blunt. I would just make dents in the table, but I would never be able to smash through."

"If I gave you a nail," I asked, "Could you hammer the nail through the table?"

"Sure," he laughed, "That's obvious."

I went on to explain that the problems he was working on were so complicated that no matter how much sound and fury he put into attacking them, he would never solve any of them if he worked on all of them at once. "Pick one, and pound the nail through the table," I told him.

Chasing Squirrels Is Fun

Later in his career, Flexner lost his focus and became famous for chasing distractions. When the renowned Gest collection of Chinese manuscripts came up for sale, Flexner scraped together funds so that he could purchase it for the IAS. The problem was that the IAS did not have a single expert in Chinese studies, and no plans to expand in that direction.

Flexner told the IAS board that that this was a once in a lifetime opportunity, and he predicted that there would be an increasing interest in China in the twentieth century. His prediction became reality fifteen years later, when Mao led a Communist takeover of China, but the IAS never developed any Chinese scholars, and Flexner spent a large fraction of the endowment of the IAS on a moonshot that was clearly outside the focus of the IAS.

The cost of this collection to the IAS was high, given that funds were tight at that time, and this purchase forced him to break his promises to some of the women and junior faculty to raise their salaries. While it was fascinating to organize the purchase of such a renowned collection of antiquities, it did Flexner's organization little long-term good.

The problem with chasing squirrels is that it is a great deal of fun. Distractions are almost always more exciting at first than what you are currently working on. They are new and appealing. It is always easier to chase a distraction than to work through a roadblock on the current project.

Deciding What Not to Do

When Flexner worked at the Rockefeller Foundation, the president of the Foundation decided to give many small grants, instead of a few large grants that could be transformative to entire institutions. Flexner said this would so dilute the mission of the Foundation that it would have little impact, and he was likely right. The early days of the Rockefeller Foundation led to the establishment of the University of Chicago and Rockefeller University, both home to multiple Nobel laureates. One could argue that nothing the Foundation did after that was as productive.

Whenever starting a new project, one of the hardest decisions a leader faces is not what to do first, it is what not to do. Many scientists fall in love with their own ideas. It takes the steel of a divorce lawyer to get them to discard any of them.

Focus means sacrifice. For everything you focus on, you do not do something else. There are opportunity costs for every decision you make. Jony Ive, the chief designer at Apple, said, "What focus means is saying no to something that with every bone in your body you think is a phenomenal idea, and you wake up thinking about it, but you end up saying no to it because you are focusing on something else."[3]

A genius can embrace the beauty of her equations, but a leader needs to be careful to avoid falling in love with the beauty of any specific idea, because that beauty might be a mirage. If you cannot envision a way to translate the idea into reality, the idea might not be worth pursuing.

"Invention is different from innovation," Lawrence Husik, a patent attorney, who teaches at Johns Hopkins, told me. "Invention is new stuff, innovation is new stuff that creates value." Your job is getting a genius to focus more on innovating and less on inventing.

Distractions Cause Arguments

Running off after a squirrel means a change in direction. If you as leader have made promises to go in the former direction, by changing directions, you break those promises. Broken promises are one of the consequences of chasing squirrels.

Flexner's chair of the Department of Mathematics at the IAS, Oswald Veblen, was persuasive, headstrong, unyielding, and thought he always knew best. Since he often ran off on tangents, he frequently broke agreements with Flexner and Einstein. He did so because he became addicted to a new idea, not for its merit, but for its novelty. He would then redirect resources promised to others, including Einstein, to his new idea.

Though Flexner had envisioned a research institute at which faculty was not wrapped up in teaching students, Veblen began to accept graduate students. He enjoyed interacting with students, because he could assign them to pursue his many ideas. So, Veblen took on graduate students, despite his agreement with Flexner not to hire any.

Flexner met with Veblen to remind him to their original agreement. Veblen proceeded to go around Flexner to the IAS faculty, which backfired, because the faculty backed Flexner. Flexner repeatedly had to steer Veblen back to the mission of the IAS: focused research without teaching. The political turmoil occurred in part because Veblen liked distractions. He liked to have many people working on several of his ideas at once.

Einstein's Focus

"We are slaves of bathrooms, Frigidaires, cars, radios, and millions of other things," said Leopold Infeld, a colleague of Einstein's at the IAS.[4] Einstein thoroughly believed this and scaled back everything in his life. He did without socks, without haircuts, and without pajamas.

His office was especially cluttered, because cleaning it up would waste precious time and, more important, it took up his attention.

Einstein's second wife, Elsa Lowenthal, did everything for him, so he could focus on his work. She asked nothing of him in return. They were with another couple one evening, when the wife asked her husband to get her coat for her. Elsa was shocked. "I would never ask the Professor to do that," she said.[5]

When Elsa passed away from heart and kidney failure, Einstein wandered through their house like a lost little boy. He had been so focused on his work he had no idea how to run a household.

Einstein was so prone to daydreaming that he would forget his way home from work. On one occasion, he called the Princeton dean's office and asked if the receptionist knew where Dr. Einstein lived. She replied that they did not give out that information. He explained that he was Dr. Einstein, and he had lost his way home.

Einstein and Elsa bought a small house in Princeton, at 112 Mercer Street, close enough to the IAS that he could walk to work when the weather permitted. His walks became an iconic fixture at Princeton. He would stroll down the sidewalks of the tree-shaded streets, lost in thought. He said he did much of his best work during those walks. He was so focused on the experiments in his head that he often would not notice any of his surroundings.

Tourists recognized him on his walks home from work. They approached him and sometimes asked to take a photo with him. He would graciously stop and oblige them, then stroll on without a word, as if no interruption had ever occurred, as if he never was aware that the tourists had been present.

Daydreaming about Physics

Einstein was notoriously addicted to distractions. His daydreaming as a patent clerk in Zurich led to the special theory of relativity, so it is difficult to think any supervisor would want to force him back on task. Einstein never saw a speaking engagement he did not want to accept, even if it was scheduled during the time he was supposed to be working at the IAS. After he accepted the appointment at the IAS, he asked to split his employment with Caltech. Flexner was appalled and worried, but he responded in an even tone, saying that for the IAS to grow it needed all of Einstein's talents. He added that Einstein would be more productive if he stayed in one place working on one project.

Flexner was right. The IAS needed Einstein for its public credibility, for philanthropy, and for further recruitment of scientists, though it is possible that Einstein might have been more productive at Caltech. He would have worked with the physicists Millikan and Feynman, instead of being isolated and ostracized by the IAS mathematicians.

Einstein had an embarrassing distraction in 1941, during the darkest days of World War II, with his involvement with the eccentric psychiatrist Wilhelm Reich. Reich wrote Einstein that he had discovered a "biologically effective energy" distinct from all current forms of energy that might be "used in the fight against the Fascist pestilence."[6] Reich claimed that he had not published this finding, because he had "bad experiences" with traditional physical scientists.

Anyone else would have been suspicious of an infinite bio-psychological energy that had never been discovered, but Einstein had discovered an infinite new energy source with his $E=mc^2$. Mass could be turned into energy. This led to the splitting of uranium into two smaller atoms whose total mass was less than the parent atom, releasing an enormous amount of energy that resulted in an atomic explosion. In addition, Einstein desperately wanted to win the war against the Nazis.

They met several times at Einstein's house in Princeton and talked for hours. They corresponded for several years. Einstein built an experimental apparatus to test Reich's energy source and found a simple electromagnetic explanation. After explaining to Reich that there was nothing extraordinary behind his theory, Einstein thought that was the end of the affair.

Reich went on to privately print a book he called *The Einstein Affair*, in which he described their discussions and correspondence and implied that Einstein supported his theory. Though Einstein responded that Reich's "theory has not my confidence,"[7] he was tainted by this charlatan science. Other physicists at Princeton snickered behind his back.

The Billion-Dollar Distraction

Forcing geniuses to focus exclusively on previously set goals means that they can miss astounding breakthroughs in another area. Most breakthroughs come from a genius daydreaming about a topic tangential to the one to which they are assigned, like Einstein in the patent office.

A leader does not want to constrain the thought process of a genius. A crucial part of the work of a leader is to free the thinking of a genius. Some distractions could be the key to a major breakthrough that is worth an enormous amount of money.

Think about the major businesses that started as distractions. Starbucks started as a wholesale supplier of coffee beans and espresso equipment. Selling freshly made, hot coffee retail was an afterthought. Twitter was an experimental side project at Odeo. 3M expanded because one of their sandpaper sales representatives realized that there would be a huge market for nonpermanent adhesives. His tinkering led to masking tape, Scotch tape, and Post-it notes.

The main dilemma of leading geniuses concerns the balance between focus and freedom. A genius will accomplish more if he focuses on the project at hand, but occasionally his distractions will be valuable insights that can lead to new industries. Some squirrels are worth chasing. The key is knowing the difference.

Distraction versus Innovation

Most leaders cannot distinguish a genius's innovative idea and a productivity-robbing distraction. Genius stands in the turf between two warring armies. On one side is the deluge of worthless distractions and on the other is the innovation that will revolutionize your organization. You cannot tell beforehand which is which.

Each side is demanding the attention of geniuses. This can paralyze them and you, and productivity grinds to a halt. The challenge is how to decide which idea is an innovation and which is a costly distraction. Two thought experiments will help you to make the call:

1. **Will the person behind the idea spend her own money to engineer the idea into a real product?** When people have to spend their own resources to put the idea into practice they become harsher critics.

2. **Does the idea enhance your core mission?** Does the new idea take what you are currently doing to the next level? By selling hot coffee in retail shops, Starbucks found the best possible customer for its coffee beans and espresso machines—itself. Starbucks's core mission was to promote coffee drinking. Their immediate project goal was to sell more espresso machines and high-quality coffee beans. Selling specialty coffees made to order in retail locations did not immediately fulfill that project goal, but it did fulfill their core mission. Ultimately, it fulfilled that prior goal, as they sold their own coffee beans at their retail locations.

Odeo was founded on the principle of increasing interpersonal connectivity. Twitter did that better than any of their other efforts. Odeo realized that Twitter fulfilled their own core mission better than anything else they were doing, so they embraced it. Odeo was able to prioritize the core mission over any single project.

Five Questions to Help You Choose Winning Ideas

Five questions can help you and a genius assess whether an idea is worth pursuing. The questions are illustrated in the diagram that follows.

1. **Is the approach innovative?** The problem may be one that has been attacked many times before, but if the approach is not novel, the idea is unlikely to succeed. An unoriginal approach will not succeed, because intellectual property may already exist. You could be doing someone else's work for them. Jac Nickoloff, a laboratory investigator, made the wry observation that a whole month of experiments could be saved by searching the Internet for one afternoon. You would be surprised by how much effort goes into repeating experiments that have already been demonstrated to fail. You can find the failures, if you spend the time to look, which was why Einstein published negative results. A closed door is still important data to others.

2. **Is the idea feasible?** The new idea can be at the edge of possibility, but it must be possible. For example, a voyage to Mars is possible, but Venus has an atmosphere of sulfuric acid heated to 870° F, hot enough to melt lead. If someone in my department proposes the equivalent of going to Venus, I am unlikely to sanction the experiment.

3. **Can your organization afford the idea?** Unless your organization has a backer like Bill Gates, you must choose ideas that can be explored with the resources you have. You can bet everything on the idea as Raytheon did with microwaves. If you cannot get enough data to obtain further funding when you expend everything you have, that single idea could kill your organization.

4. **Is the idea specific enough not to impair other efforts?** Exploring the idea must come with low opportunity costs. If the idea leads to a dead end, the original project must not be irreparably damaged. No one should be fired because your team explored a novel idea.

5. **Is the idea elegant?** How do you assess the elegance of an idea? There are two different types of elegance. One is what I call smacked-forehead elegance. When an idea is explained to you, you smack your forehead and say, "Of course! I should have thought of that!" The approach is novel yet understood by the entire team, not just the genius. Everyone sees right away how the idea would work. The idea is like a good joke. Everyone gets it, and it brings smiles to their faces.

The other type of elegance is other-worldly. It is like an eclipse of the sun. It makes you feel small in the face of the universe. The reaction to this type of elegance is awe at the magnitude of the insight. There is a sense of the sacred. The idea is beyond the team's normal capacity, and the team is grateful they are part of it. The proposed idea is met with the same jaw-dropping wonder as walking into the Sistine Chapel.

The sacred elegance of this type of idea can take root in your heart and be hard to let go of if it fails. The awe inspired by the insight should not be mistaken for the potential for application. This type of elegance can be beguiling. Both genius and leader can marry these ideas and live with them through sickness and health, regardless of whether they actually help the organization. It is the leader's job to help the genius get past the beauty of their equations to what actually helps the team. See Figure 9.1 (next page).

Once again, balance becomes paramount in leading genius. Allowing a genius to pursue every distraction leads to a diffusion of the core mission and a loss of team cohesion. Not only does the original project not get finished, but the genius never catches any of the ideas she has chased.

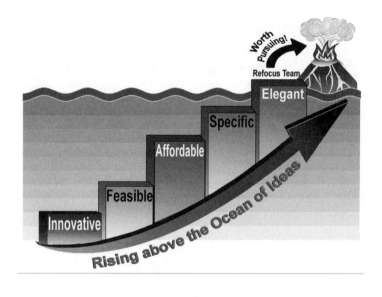

On the other hand, too much forced focus constrains the creative talent of geniuses, and they cannot make any breakthroughs. Using the five questions discussed above to test ideas before exploring them can be an exercise in focus in itself, as you carefully choose which to explore. These questions will help you to identify the idea that is translatable to the market.

A genius is easily distracted away from the project, just by nature of his genius. No matter how smart he is, he cannot study everything. Since some distractions lead to entirely new industries, choosing which distraction to pursue is perhaps the most important decision any leader can make.

CRUCIAL TAKE-AWAY:

A good leader ignores squirrels; a great leader carefully chooses which to chase.

RULE 8:
HARMONIZE HEARTS
AND MINDS

10

No matter what we think, no matter how hard we try to be stoic and professional, our emotions can control our lives and the life of a genius. For a genius to be most productive, his heart needs to be in harmony with his mind. If his heart is troubled, the mind of a genius will be distracted and uncreative. His intellect will be caught up in the turmoil of emotions, unable to roam freely across the landscape of his imagination.

Understanding this, Flexner could be very compassionate. Perhaps the best example of this is his patient pursuit of the famed German mathematical physicist Hermann Weyl, mentioned earlier. Weyl had a Jewish wife, whom he deeply loved. Although he was highly patriotic, he was nervous about the Nazis' rise to power. When Flexner first offered him a faculty job in 1932, Weyl was the chair of Mathematics at the University of Göttingen, widely regarded as the best mathematics group in the world. Weyl accepted Flexner's offer, then declined it, then "irrevocably" accepted it.

Flexner was thrilled, and the IAS board approved the appointment. In 1933, just before he was to move, Weyl's mother-in-law died of influenza. Weyl cabled Flexner that he felt he should stay in Germany.

Weyl explained later that he had hoped to influence the political direction Germany was taking. The Nazis swept to power despite his efforts. Weyl was naïve in the extreme to think he could alter their push to power. Caught between the love for his university and country and his love for his wife, he developed severe depression and was hospitalized in Zurich.

The IAS board was insulted by Weyl's rejection. They annulled his faculty appointment. Instead, they gave Weyl's position to John von Neumann, who played the key role in the development of computers, as mentioned earlier.

During Weyl's hospitalization, the Nazis dismissed the Jewish faculty at Göttingen, and most of the remaining faculty resigned in protest. Having returned to the decimated Göttingen math program, Weyl agonized over the danger to his wife. He realized that he would have to leave Germany to save her, but he might have waited too long.

He contacted multiple universities, but there were no positions, because so many qualified scientists were fleeing Germany. He had kept in contact with Veblen, who with others mentioned to Flexner that Weyl was becoming desperate for his wife's safety.

Flexner generously offered Weyl another position, and Weyl immediately accepted. Weyl and his family were able to leave Germany without the Nazis becoming aware of the offer. Three years later, Weyl wrote to Flexner, "Each year when we are leaving Princeton [for summer vacation], Mrs. Weyl and I realize anew how much we owe to you, dear Dr. Flexner."[1]

Flexner understood that Weyl's conflicting emotions, duty to his university, patriotism for his country, and love for his wife, constrained him from acting rationally. Flexner understood that a genius is first a human, and second a genius.

Flexner did not hold a grudge against Weyl for turning him down. His ability to let go of Weyl's past rejection probably saved Weyl's wife from the Holocaust. His unusual generosity and forgiveness allowed Flexner to maintain a relationship with Weyl even after Weyl had changed his mind and rejected the IAS.

Alone on Friday Night

Late one Friday night, I was about to leave our medical center complex, when I saw one of my most famous cardiology faculty, who had assisted in inventing a new heart valve replacement, in scrubs in the ER. I knew he had been on call the previous night. I asked him why he was still there.

"I had a big fight with my wife. I just don't know how to talk to her anymore, and I would rather be at the hospital than at home," he answered.

Whoa, that was not the right answer on so many levels. I stopped and sat down with him. I tried to explain that in doing this much night call he was doing his patients no favors. Also, by working long hours, he was putting more relational distance between him and his wife. He would not resolve their argument by avoiding her. Silence just postpones arguments, it does not resolve them.

We talked about how fatigue would cause him to lose his creative edge, and he would end up just going through the motions. Patients came to him because he came up with innovative ways to treat their heart disease. If he had issues at home and stayed at the hospital to avoid the pain of resolving their marriage conflicts, he would be too distracted and tired to be the physician his patients needed him to be. His patients needed his genius to survive, and he would not be focused enough on them to help. He sighed, and decided to go back home that night. That led to an agreement to seek counseling, and restored the harmony of his heart with his intellect.

Genius Needs a Team

The great advances today are most commonly made with teams of multiple true geniuses supported by many others. The lone genius working behind a closed door in a dark basement office making a great technological advance is almost unheard of anymore. In the past, a genius could hide a dysfunctional personality, because he was alone most of the time. Newton by most accounts was a harsh and angry person, but he worked alone using a mathematical system which allowed him to do that.

Today, advances in physics are made by huge teams of geniuses, each with a tiny but deep piece of the problem. Anger, bullying, and selfishness cannot be hidden in this situation, and any one of those qualities would wreck the team. Given that most geniuses have to work closely with others to make real advances today, communication, honesty, and caring for the team are more important than ever. These characteristics all stem more from the heart than the mind.

A genius must have within herself a passion that can be ignited. Your job is to provide the spark that lights that passion. To succeed, geniuses must have character, and you as their leader must be able to reach inside them to touch that character.

The great leaps that genius can make require the genius to care about the problem deeply and emotionally. Geniuses require the freedom to think any thought, no matter how dangerous or how absurd. This freedom only comes when a genius is in a warm and supportive environment, in which there is little cost to thinking radical thoughts.

Galileo was much less productive after he was shown the instruments that would torture him if he continued to study how the Earth revolves around the sun. Einstein's major creative burst, nearly unequaled in history, came when he was a patent clerk in Zurich, surrounded by friends, and still in the midst of a warm, passionate love affair with Mileva, his first wife.

Listening to Mary

Robert Cade—the inventor of Gatorade—was an example of a happy genius. He would have been the first to admit that his best discoveries came from discussing them with his wife, Mary, who knew nothing about kidney function, his specialty.

When he took a break from work, he would walk over to the practice field to watch the University of Florida Gators summer football practices. Summer in Florida feels like someone dropped a hot wet blanket over your head. You cannot breathe, and you sweat profusely, but the sweat never evaporates. The football players drank gallons of water every practice, but Cade noticed that they did not urinate afterwards. He asked the now famous question, "Why don't football players wee-wee after practice?"[2]

Having scraped the sweat of football players and analyzed what salts they were losing, he found that football players lost as much as eighteen pounds of fluid during one game, and that they lost not only sodium but also potassium. Since drinking water was not enough to maintain blood volume and stamina during the game, he realized that football players need to replenish sodium and potassium as well as water, and they needed glucose to absorb these salts.

Excited by the prospect of giving the Florida football team an edge up on the opposition, Cade and his team created the first sports replacement drink, and tested it on the freshman football players. Although it seemed to work in maintaining the players' stamina, none of them wanted to drink it, because "it sort of tasted like toilet-bowl cleaner," Dana Shires, one of Cade's team members told me.

One evening, Cade mentioned to his wife Mary that he could not get the players to drink enough of his drink to replenish their lost fluids, because it tasted so bad. She came up with the idea of adding a grocery-store lemonade mixture, and Gatorade was born!

Gatorade first made a difference in the 1965 Florida football game against LSU. Playing in 102-degree weather, the LSU team faded badly in the second half, but the fortified Gators did not. They came back and won the game. The Florida football coach was convinced that Gatorade made the difference, and he asked Cade and his team to generate enough for the whole team for the rest of the season.

The Gators cemented their national reputation as a team that never faded when they came from behind to win the 1967 Orange Bowl against Georgia Tech. Bobby Dodd, the Georgia Tech coach, asked to explain the loss at the press conference after the game, said "We didn't have Gatorade."[3]

My former department and the University of Florida still benefits from Cade's persistent genius. The royalties from the copyright of the name have run into billions of dollars. Those royalties have gone to support biomedical research and training young scientists in kidney disease.

Though Dr. Cade passed away in 2007, his wife Mary still attended most of our university social functions. At a huge banquet celebrating the anniversary of Gatorade, I leaned over and said to her, "Without you this would not have happened."

She laughed and said, "Of course, it would have. Somebody else would have done it."

I do not agree. Much of genius is making the unseen obvious. Mary contributed just as much to the multi-billion-dollar enterprise as Bob did. He went most of the way up the mountain, but she pushed him over the top. I am convinced that Bob Cade's relationship with Mary allowed him to achieve more than he could have done if he had been alone. Mary gave him the support and freedom to be creative. She paid attention to Bob when he talked about problems at work. She practiced active listening without even knowing what it was. Bob flourished because of the supportive emotional environment he was in.

I often wonder how many geniuses leaders miss because the genius is not in the right emotional environment. A great leader recognizes genius, and then provides the most secure and empowering emotional environment he can, specific to that genius. A great leader discovers and develops genius.

Einstein's Love Affairs

Even Einstein was susceptible to emotions that drove him to behave uncharacteristically and limited his productivity. In 1905, Einstein came up with his quantum theory of the photoelectric effect, which led to his Nobel Prize and his theory of special relativity, the famous $E=mc^2$. He called this time period his *Annus Mirabilis*, his miracle year, because he had so many insights he could not catalogue them all.

Fantastic ideas tumbled out of his brain one after another as fast he could scribble them down on his index cards at his desk in the Bern patent office. He was in awe of the insights. He loved the beauty of the mathematical equations, and how it opened up the universe. This miracle year occurred when he was passionately in love with Mileva Maric, a physics student he had met at the University of Bern.

As he daydreamed and scribbled on index cards at his desk at work, he had what he later called "the most fortunate thought of my life."[4] Einstein envisioned a man falling from a building, and the relationship of that man to an object he dropped after he had fallen. He used this image to build his theory of special relativity as applied to gravity.

Contrast this astounding burst of creativity to a decade later when his and Mileva's marriage was falling apart. They were constantly fighting, as he became increasingly famous. The demands of his career cut into his time with his family. Every interaction between him and his wife was filled with tension and bitterness.

Einstein agreed to try to maintain the marriage for the sake of their children. Ever the scientist, he made a set of detailed demands to stay in the marriage that boggle the mind. He stipulated that she clean his room, bring three meals a day up to him, and renounce all personal conversation and intimacy. She was not to expect Einstein to spend any time with her or to accompany her on any errand. She had to stop talking when he told her to.

He was remorseful at times about his demands. "We men are deplorable, dependent creatures," he wrote to his friend Michele Besso.[5]

When Mileva and Einstein separated, Besso tried to intervene and save the marriage. After visiting Mileva in Zurich in 1916, he wrote to Einstein asking him to try for a reconciliation during the summer break. Einstein would have none of it.

"I would have been physically and mentally broken if I had not finally found the strength to keep her at arm's length," he wrote back.[6]

Einstein eventually divorced Mileva with the promise that he would leave her his money from the Nobel Prize. He married his distant cousin, Elsa Lowenthal in 1919. She ran his household, paid the bills, kept his schedule, and most of all never complained. She never asked anything of him and was content to bask in his shadow.

Their marriage was thought to be mainly platonic after the first few years. Einstein is believed to have had multiple affairs during the marriage. He probably had an affair with his secretary, Betty Neumann. He was a charismatic cultural icon who attracted many women, not just fellow scientists. In a book of his letters, Einstein described six women with whom he likely had affairs.[7]

Elsa apparently did not mind. She kept the 112 Mercer Street house in Princeton for him. She allowed him the same freedom in their marriage that he had at the IAS.

As Einstein grew older, he became famous for his generosity and gentleness. His harsh parameters for his marriage with Mileva were so uncharacteristic of him. His behavior demonstrated that the pressures and tensions of the heart can make even the greatest minds behave badly. Even a genius with a good character can be tormented by emotions and driven to do brutal things. The heart affects what the brain does, and none of us can ever get around that, not even Einstein.

The Emotional Environment Shapes Genius

When he worked at the patent office, Einstein had friends and a positive, accepting environment in Bern. His supervisor there, the genial Friedrich Haller, let Einstein scribble away on his note cards without interference. Einstein later said, "[I] hatched my most beautiful ideas" there.[8] One of Einstein's friends in Bern, Marcel Grossman, a wealthy college classmate, let Einstein study for exams using his notes, because Einstein had skipped class so often. When Einstein finished his studies at the University of Bern and needed work, Grossman got him the job in the patent office.

Michel Besso, whom Einstein considered his best friend, provided emotional support for Einstein. He urged Einstein to read the empirical philosopher Ernst Mach, who argued that only conclusions based on experiments or mathematical analysis could be trusted.

Einstein admired Mach's "incorruptible skepticism."[9] He modeled his own cheerful skepticism on this empirical philosophy, and never let his ego get in the way of admitting that he was wrong. He always tested his own assumptions carefully.

Working at the patent office played a significant role in the development of Einstein's genius. Although the work was boring, it required careful attention to detail and a prodigious memory, because patents could not infringe on another. Knowledge of engineering and math was needed for the job. Working at the patent office trained Einstein's mind to think carefully and logically.

The only surviving patent evaluation from Einstein comes from a court document dated 1907. The Bern patent office destroyed the rest of his work after Einstein achieved his global celebrity. In the only surviving evaluation, he rejected a patent by the AEG Company of Berlin for an alternating-current machine, because it was "incorrectly, imprecisely, and not clearly prepared."[10] Precision would become a trademark of Einstein.

By getting the tedious work of the patent office done fast, he was able to spend much of his day writing out mathematical equations on small index cards, which he stashed in his desk whenever a supervisor walked by. The patent office job not only trained him to think rigorously, which given Einstein's lackadaisical approach to life was something he needed, but the job also gave him the opportunity to think unfettered and uninterrupted while getting paid for it.

Since he had not yet completed his Ph.D. program, the preconceptions and models that dominated academic physics at that time did not constrain him. He essentially had a paid research position before he ever joined the faculty of a university. He probably had fewer interruptions in his patent office than at any other time in his career.

This supportive environment allowed Einstein's genius to flourish. We take for granted that a genius is born with innate intelligence beyond the rest of us, but we fail to take into account the role of their environment in allowing genius to flourish.

Internal Consistency

The ultimate goal in caring for the hearts of geniuses is to guide them to internal consistency. Their hearts and brains must be aligned. No one, not even a genius, does well when the emotions and the intellect are not in harmony. The resulting cognitive dissonance can be a powerful and painful force, powerful because it can change the behavior of the strongest intellect, and painful because it can hurt a genius so badly that she avoids certain challenges that you might need her to take on.

Cognitive dissonance can make a genius do strange things, which can disrupt the team. Caring for the heart of a genius means helping him toward a state of internal consistency, in which his emotions and intellect are correctly aligned. This is the sweet spot for creativity.

People go to great lengths to maintain consistency between their internal and external environments. When the brain or the heart is uncomfortable with something, we try to force the other into some sort of consistency. If our emotions tell us we want something that we know we cannot have, then we make up reasons why we do not really want it in the first place.

A well-known experiment testing cognitive dissonance demonstrated that we lie to ourselves in order to avoid cognitive dissonance. The experiment took two groups of people and had them do a boring task.[11] The first group of people was paid $20, the second group $1. Both groups had to convince another person that the task was fun after they had performed the task and knew it was boring. After trying to convince the other person, both groups were asked to rate whether the task was actually fun or not. The group paid $20 rated the task as boring, but the group paid $1 rated the task as fun.

The psychologists, who did the study, proposed that the lower-paid group rated the task as fun because they needed internal consistency in order to convince another person that the task was fun. The discomfort of cognitive dissonance compelled them to lie to themselves that the task was fun in order to lie to the other person. Since the higher-paid group was paid well to lie, they did not need any internal reason to lie.

Cognitive dissonance is a problem for a genius. A genius will seek internal harmony, even if it means convincing himself of things that are not really true. A genius has to alter the way he sees reality in order to maintain internal harmony. Doing this inserts an essential flaw, a computer worm, into the thought process of a genius.

Disharmony between the hearts and minds of geniuses will produce an internal dissonance that will subvert their intellectual capabilities. For them to tolerate cognitive dissonance, they will convince themselves of untruths. Allowing that mental sloppiness to exist in even a corner of their minds will slice off mental strength from their creativity.

A disharmony between mind and heart, between intellect and emotions can occur from an unhappy love affair or from the lack of support from their leader. Dissonance can occur if the heart of a genius is seduced by power or wealth, causing the genius to misbehave. In this circumstance, the heart of a genius drives the intellect to do things the intellect knows are counter-productive.

No matter how much a genius is aware that these actions will harm her in the long run, she cannot stop, because she has allowed a lie to live within her mind. She has accepted a falsehood in order to maintain cognitive consonance.

Methods for Resolving Internal Dissonance

Resolving the dissonance derived from a misalignment of emotions with intellect takes time and patience, because you have to first build a relationship with a genius to be able to identify areas of disharmony. The ways to build a trusting relationship are as follows:

- Your own self-assessment is a crucial first step to avoid being self-centered, so that you are sensitive to what is going on inside a genius. Self-assessment makes you more accessible emotionally for your genius.

- Active listening allows you to talk about the issues bothering a genius before they become disastrous. Since geniuses are busy, scheduling this time is a good idea. I always serve something to drink—coffee or diet sodas—because the physiological act of swallowing slows the heart rate and decreases tension.

I ask tangential questions to avoid creating defensiveness. Instead of asking a genius about his relationship with his spouse, I ask whether they are getting enough romantic weekends away. Instead of inquiring about how their children are behaving, I ask whether the genius is happy with his children's school. Open the topic with a question that is nonthreatening, and then use the read-back and follow-up of active listening to probe deeper.

- *Your transparency is important in establishing the trust required for a genius to open up about the issues bothering her.* Unless a genius can trust that you do not have a hidden agenda except her welfare, she will not open up to you about issues that are constricting her creativity.

- *Promoting the alchemy of team relationships helps a genius to not feel isolated.* By putting the right mix of personalities together, you can create many opportunities for a genius to open up about the stressors they face.

Take the time to look at the life of a genius. Leaders avoid doing this, because they think it will be a black hole for their time and energy. I contend that if you do not, you will pay far more in terms of lost productivity later.

Look for signs of disharmony in geniuses. Observe if they are distracted or edgy. Are they easily angered or irritated all the time? Are they unusually argumentative and obstructionist? These are signs of misalignment between the heart and mind. I call this emotional disintegration, as the illustration below shows. If the heart and mind

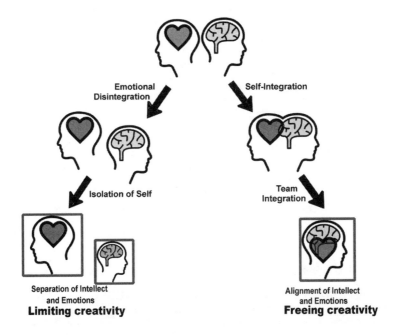

are not aligned, then the emotions will be inconsistent with what the genius is thinking. See Figure 10.1.

It is as if his heart and mind are speaking different languages. The heart and mind do not understand each other, which will result in disintegration. In many instances, geniuses may deny to themselves that this disintegration is happening, because of the pain of cognitive dissonance. Your job is to help her see this deception for what it is.

Next, the genius will isolate herself from the rest of the team. Her creativity will be limited, because she cannot focus on the problem. Only the self-integrated genius, with heart and mind aligned, can integrate with the team.

You should consider the time spent providing tools for a genius to integrate his heart and mind an investment in your team, because the payoff is increased creativity. The emotions motivate the mind and can guide pathways of discovery. The elegance of a breakthrough can first appeal to the heart. Einstein himself felt that the beauty of his equations called to him through the fog of the unknown.

Sometimes a leader will have little to offer to help. The genius may have an intractable problem, say a child with cancer, which you cannot fix. At that moment, the only thing the leader can do is to stand with the genius and share her suffering. This does not make it easier for the genius, but it makes it less lonely.

One of the division chiefs under me lost a daughter to leukemia several years ago. The faculty in his division covered his night and weekend hospital calls, so that he did not have to be away from home any more than necessary. These faculty helped him create a charity for treating children with cancer in the Dominican Republic, named the Keira Grace Foundation after his daughter. He has been forever grateful to those faculty members, and this led to an even better integration with his team.

Supporting geniuses as they suffer life's reverses creates a relationship that is difficult to break. Before there was paid sick leave, when I was about five, my father had rheumatic fever and was out of work for six months. His employer made sure he stayed on the payroll and allowed him to come back to work slowly, so that he could regain his strength. The employer's generosity created a loyalty that persisted, and my father stayed with that employer the rest of his career.

Caring for the heart of a genius can do that as well. Generosity breeds loyalty, and loyalty is key to maintaining stable teams.

CRUCIAL TAKE-AWAY

Geniuses create with their hearts just as much as their heads.

RULE 9:
LET THE PROBLEM SEDUCE THE GENIUS

11

Getting a genius to work on a project the organization needs, rather than on what he wants is a big challenge for a leader of genius. Anyone with the deep focus of a genius has a high energy of activation for any new project. It takes a lot of energy to get them to stop what they are doing to start working on a new project, even if it is highly interesting. Getting geniuses to do something they do not want to do is even harder.

Geniuses can have fifty great reasons why they should do what they want to do and not what you want. Since they are smarter than you, these reasons are usually more rational and cohesive than yours. Since the new project is ultimately more important, you are likely correct, but convincing a genius of that is difficult. For the good of the organization, you must be able to redirect the genius on your team.

Your job as leader is to let the problem seduce a genius by presenting the goal as a solution or product that does not yet exist. If one of the definitions of genius is to make the unseen visible and the unimagined possible, your job is to make geniuses believe the project involves something unseen that is waiting to be discovered. Dwight Eisenhower said, "Motivation is the art of getting people to do what you want them to do, because they want to do it."[1]

Flexner had great powers of passion. When Bamberger and colleagues first met with Flexner about how to spend their fortune, they wanted to endow a medical school in Newark for Jewish students. Flexner believed that the New York City region already had a number of medical schools that accepted Jewish students. Instead, Flexner asked them, "Have you ever dreamed a dream?"[2] He then proceeded to outline his plan for the Institute for Advanced Study, and the Bambergers were caught up in that vision.

Strategic Vision as Enticement

A leader's most powerful motivational tool is to tantalize a genius with the problem. By 1930, Einstein had decided that he did not have a future in Germany because of the rise of the Nazis, and he entertained offers from Madrid, Paris, Leiden, Oxford, Turkey, Hebrew University, and the California Institute of Technology (Caltech). Although Einstein was being pursued by much more famous institutions all over the world, he chose Flexner and the IAS, because of the vision Flexner communicated.

Robert Millikan, the president of Caltech, had been trying to hire Einstein for years. Millikan had built a formidable mathematics and physics department in a relatively short time. He had won the Nobel Prize for his experiments proving Einstein's 1905 hypothesis that light is a particle. At the time, the IAS was nothing but an idea in Flexner's mind, an idea supported by the Bamberger fortune. Einstein was ensconced as a guest professor at Caltech when Flexner visited Millikan to discuss his ideas for the IAS.

Flexner said he would never have presumed to offer a job to the most famous scientist in the world. Both Flexner and Einstein were Millikan's guests, and Millikan was also trying to recruit Einstein to Caltech. It would have been socially awkward for Flexner to make an offer to Einstein while being Millikan's guest.

Einstein resolved the problem by making the first move at Caltech, contacting Flexner first. Once the door was opened, Flexner pursued the opportunity doggedly. At their first meeting, Flexner said he was fascinated by Einstein's noble bearing, and "his simple, charming manner, and his genuine humility."[3] They spoke for more than an hour, pacing up and down the hallways at Caltech. Einstein had to be reminded three times that he had another appointment before he pulled himself away.

A few months later, Flexner visited Einstein at Oxford, where they spent most of the day walking through the campus, conversing about Flexner's vision for the IAS. During this conversation, Flexner offered him a position with whatever terms Einstein wanted. Einstein was noncommittal.

During his courtship of Einstein, Flexner also offered a position to George Birkhoff, a Harvard mathematician. After accepting the position in writing and just before he was to start, Birkhoff announced publicly that he was staying at Harvard. His actions damaged the credibility of the IAS for Flexner's other recruits. Angry that Birkhoff had made his rejection public, Flexner outwardly maintained his enthusiastic vision for the IAS. Instead of retaliating against Birkhoff, he focused on recruiting Einstein.

Flexner and Einstein could not have been more different. Flexner was neat, intense, organized, monogamous, and doted on his children. Einstein was disheveled, gentle, disorganized, polyamorous, and had little to do with his children. Yet Einstein resonated with Flexner's vision for the cloistered, research-based IAS. The vision was seductive.

Flexner traveled to Einstein's country home in Germany, where he reiterated his offer. This time Einstein agreed to send his terms to Flexner. Einstein reportedly told Flexner that he was "on fire with the idea." Flexner's efforts had paid off. He returned to the United States with Einstein's commitment to join the IAS, which he used to shore up the Bambergers' flagging support at the start of the Great Depression.

Flexner had two advantages in his negotiations with Einstein. He could offer a higher salary than anyone else, and he communicated a compelling vision for the IAS. Millikan was miffed that Einstein joined the IAS instead of Caltech. He complained to Flexner that he had stolen Einstein. Millikan appealed to Flexner to allow Einstein to spend half his time at Caltech, because Einstein's area of physics was far more developed at Caltech. Einstein may have been more creative at Caltech, but Millikan was also militaristic and nationalistic, two characteristics Einstein abhorred. In fact, Millikan had recently taken a large contribution from a Nazi sympathizer with the stipulation that there would be no anti-German activities at Caltech. If Einstein had known about that exchange, their relationship would have been shattered. Millikan lost out on recruiting Einstein, because he failed to communicate a vision to Einstein that had an impact on Einstein's imagination.

Individual Enticements

Flexner's recruitment of Einstein involved subtle aspects as well. He understood that Einstein liked natural settings and solitude. He painted a picture of the IAS as a country retreat where scientists could pursue their research without the bustle of big city crowds, students, and the interruptions that come with a large university. The village of Princeton was set amid farmland and woods, where Einstein could take long, quiet walks. Einstein loved to sail, and he could keep his small boat nearby which would allow him to spend many hours on the water.

Einstein was constantly in demand as a speaker, and many other institutions tried to lure him away from the IAS, but Princeton became the place where he most thought himself at home. Flexner understood Einstein's unspoken longing to be alone and outdoors in a natural setting when no one else did.

Money and Motivation

Most organizations operate with the idea that employees will work as hard as you compensate them. This compensation can be in many forms, not just salaries. Job security, perquisites within the company, and external status are all forms of compensation.

Although compensation can incentivize employees, salary and benefits should not be mistaken for motivation. Motivation includes a broader sense of purpose for making a difference. A genius chooses a job as much for motivation as for compensation. Compensation without motivation leads to burnout and job-hopping.

If a genius feels that she is not fairly compensated, then that feeling will become an irritating distraction. She will feel taken advantage of and become irritated. But money does not drive most genius. Although compensation rarely motivates geniuses, they can be distracted by poor compensation, when it is not sufficient to make them comfortable.

Money was a wonderful motivator in the Industrial Age, when workers performed manual tasks in factories in a mindless manner. Tasks have since changed for people. Robots do most of the mindless factory work. The majority of discoveries now are theoretical at first. It may take years before there is a practical application of the discovery.

Flexner recognized this lag in his article, "The Usefulness of Useless Knowledge."[5] He proposed that since no one knows which discoveries will be translated into wide public use, research should be supported for its own sake.

For most leaders, our comfort zone lies in compensation. Leaders have been trained from our first management classes on the uses of compensation. A leader of genius needs to provide enough compensation so that money is not a worry to the genius. This frees a genius to focus on his project without the irritation that might throw him off track.

One way to take compensation off the table is to pay geniuses more than they think they are worth. Einstein asked for a salary that was lower than what Flexner intended to pay. During his final recruitment meeting with Einstein, Flexner had to convince Einstein to take more money. Instead of gleefully signing Einstein to a lower salary and keeping the difference, Flexner argued that Einstein should make more money, because he did not want Einstein to become unhappy with his salary later.

The Alluring Joy of Discovery

Many leaders of genius know that they cannot force a change in direction by a genius, so they use nudges. Nudges are small pushes toward a desired behavior without forbidding other options. Described by the Nobel Laureate Robert Thaler, nudging relies on appealing to fundamental desires we all have. Though most of us can be enticed by the thought of fulfilling those desires, a genius often does not share the same desires.

One of my division chiefs complained to me recently that the nudges he used never worked. He was using nudges that would have worked on himself, but were not appealing to the geniuses working for him. A genius needs unique nudges.

The joy of discovery is one desire that is overwhelming for a genius. When investigators first realize the significance of what they have discovered, they feel a high that catches them by surprise and takes their breath away. They feel gratitude as if they do not deserve it. They feel overwhelmed and invincible at the same time. Once geniuses experience that joy, they will spend the rest of their lives chasing it. Discovery is the most rewarding part of their job, and a leader can use it as a nudge.

"To myself I seem to have been only like a boy playing on the seashore, and diverting myself in now and then finding a smoother pebble or a prettier shell than ordinary, whilst the great ocean of truth lay all undiscovered before me" Newton reportedly said on his deathbed.[6]

One of the young scientists in my lab worked for three years trying to find out how an enzyme worked without any progress. One day, using a confocal microscope, she found the answer. "The hair on the back of my neck stood up when I first saw the nuclear changes," she said. "It was a feeling I will never forget."

After he won the 1981 Nobel Prize in Physics, Arthur Schawlow was asked in an interview what made the difference between a genius and a smart person. "The labor of love aspect is important," he said.

"The most successful scientists often are not the most talented. But they are the ones who are impelled by curiosity. They've got to know what the answer is."[7]

"I have no special talents. I am only passionately curious," Einstein said.[8]

Preschool Art Is the Same as a Genius at Work

An iconic psychology experiment on the importance of discovery was done in the 1970's on preschool children drawing pictures.[9] The children were separated into three groups. One group was told they would receive a blue ribbon if they drew well. Another group was told they would get nothing, but unexpectedly received a large red ribbon for drawing well. The last group was told they would get nothing, and they did not receive a reward for drawing well.

After two weeks, the children in the two groups who were told they would not receive anything continued to draw creatively and enthusiastically. The children in the blue-ribbon group lost pleasure in drawing and produced little. The extrinsic motivation had destroyed their interest in creating. Drawing became a job, and it was boring.

If the intrinsic joy of discovery drives most productivity, you have to learn to enhance the opportunities for the joy of discovery for the genius working on your team.

You have to stress the meaning of the solution. Talk to a genius about what solving the problem would mean to the world around her. Do not direct her to work on the problem. Instead, describe the difficulty of the problem and the purpose underlying the solution.

When I asked 491 medical school departmental chairs from around the country what they desired most from their leader, the most common answer was a strategic vision. They wanted to know where the organization was going and why. Presenting a strategic vision is more than providing a direction. The vision must give a purpose for that direction. Interestingly, the skill that these department chairs cared least about was financial acumen.

You have to celebrate discovery. Every year, we honor a junior and senior laboratory investigator in my department. We give a cash award and a plaque, but the most important part of the celebration is that they tell the story of their discovery. The goal is to make discovery a memorable event for the team.

Shortly after Einstein arrived at the IAS, he attended a graduate student lecture, during which the student described several simple lab experiments that proved Einstein's $E=mc^2$ equation. "Einstein had been so preoccupied with other studies that he had not realized that such confirmation of his early theories had become an everyday affair in the physical laboratory," A. E. Condon, a professor at Princeton, wrote. Einstein grinned like a small boy, and repeatedly asked, "Is it really true?"[10] That smile came from the overwhelming sense of delight at seeing his theory become real.

The Unmovable Genius

Some geniuses will resist any change, even in the face of a compelling vision for discovery. I have found that geniuses who are resistant to change fall into three major categories: the Cynic, the Fearful, and the Righteous.

The Cynic is pessimistic about the success of all new ventures, because they fear losing the safety of familiarity. They take pride in pointing out all the mistaken assumptions and pitfalls in the plan, which gives them a reason for being. They take joy in the failure of others, especially if they predicted it. Since they predict everything will fail, they are correct some of the time, and they are triumphant when that happens. Failure is a validation of their prophetic powers, even if the failure originated from their own inactivity.

The Cynic may have had a spectacular failure in the past or had been beaten by a competitor. Or the failure may have been personal or professional, a failed relationship or being removed from a leadership position. The genius may have worked all out to discover a new superconducting ceramic, only to have another group discover it first. Being second in a race, in which only the winner counts, when he gave everything he had, could make him expect that any difficult task will fail.

The way to deal with the Cynic is to use judo by employing their prophetic momentum against them. Get the Cynic to list all the problems with the new project. As her momentum reaches its peak, thank her for identifying where the work needs to start. Since a Cynic sees the issues better than anyone does, ask her to lead a group to come up with solutions to these problems. Turn her problem identification into problem resolution. When the Cynic solves the first problem, let her talk about how hard it was. Validate that it was a huge problem, and be publicly grateful that she identified it in the first place.

Another unmovable personality type is the Fearful, who prefers to keep doing what they are doing, because they are anxious about loss of belonging. They fear that failure will lead to disruption of the team, and the team fills an important need for them. They do not want the team to change directions for fear that it will leave them behind.

The Fearful are likely to be passive aggressive and avoid any overt resistance. They might say "yes" to any request to perform a task, but never get it done. This personality type is harder to identify, because the Fearful often hide behind others.

The Fearful might doubt their ability to get the job done. Since they take much of their self-esteem from their job and their team, they feel that failure will expose them as a fraud and result in their dismissal from the team. No amount of assurance that they will remain part of the team will permit them to redirect their efforts.

Flexner himself was an example of a Fearful type. When Princeton University offered the Nobel Prize-winning physicist Erwin Schrodinger a job, he turned it down, because he really wanted to work with

Einstein at the IAS. Flexner was so afraid of upsetting Princeton for hiring a candidate away from them that he turned Schrodinger away, missing an opportunity to put the two physics giants together. Schrodinger ended up at neither place. In one of the worst moves imaginable, he returned to Austria just before the Nazis invaded.

The way to deal with the Fearful personality type is to narrow the task. Give him only what he knows he can handle. This means slicing the project into small tasks, so that the Fearful can see the end result before he even starts. The entire project should be presented in incremental pieces. The Fearful need help to visualize success more than other types of genius.

A stable and fulfilling relationship with you and the team helps to provide this type of genius with a secure work environment. That means social gatherings should be regular, and interactions should always include discussions of family and hobbies.

The Righteous are the most difficult to deal with, because they are convinced that everyone else is an idiot. What makes this type even more complicated is that they are often right. They are smarter than anyone else in the room. They fear that failure will change their view of themselves, and this loss of self-esteem is psychologically unacceptable.

The fear of failure makes them arrogant and rigid. If they believe they can do no wrong, they are unreceptive to instruction. They have difficulty changing goals, if it is someone else's goal.

In the past of the Righteous, you might find one great triumph. He might have been the scientist who beat out the Cynic, but then was never able to replicate that success. He lived on that one triumph for his whole career. Being Righteous reinforces that great moment, bringing that triumph into the present.

To move the Righteous, introduce the project as a problem on which his opinion is needed. Get him to speculate on possible approaches. When he mentions the specific project the company had in mind for your team, do not seem too eager. Casually pounce on that approach and say, "Hmm, that might work, but only if you are on board and play a major role." You will be using his need to be right to pull him where you need him to be.

The Righteous also respond to scarcity and competition. If you can frame the problem as a race, then their need to be right can transform into their need to be first. I could only motivate a young woman scientist to work on something by telling her that it could not be done. She would argue with me for an hour, then spend a month of feverish work just to prove me wrong, which I was happy to admit when she did.

Captivating the Heart

If geniuses feel forced to change directions, their creativity will be constrained. There are places they cannot go in their minds. They cannot be as innovative as they would be if they were convinced from inside out, instead of forcing change from the outside in. Your goal is to captivate the heart of a genius. Persuasion cannot be external and material in nature, because attempts at persuading a genius rarely work. Making the new project attractive and letting geniuses discover the new direction for themselves is far more effective.

"I was born not knowing and have had only a little time to change that here and there," Richard Feynman said.[11]

Changing the direction of a genius is a fluid, dynamic process that takes skill and caution. The balance between too much and too little is narrow. That is why it is much better to try many small enticements. It is easier to calibrate small attractions for the right effect. This takes a lot of active listening to do correctly.

There is a momentum to this seduction as well. You may need to stop before you think you do, because the genius may already be rolling down the hill to a decision before indicating they are ready to make changes.

Geniuses immerse themselves in a project with tenacity, even if that project is unproductive. See Figure 11.1 (next page), "The Joy of Discovery."

Discovering a solution is what motivates a genius, not translating that solution to a commercial market. The barriers to changing the focus of a genius include cynicism, self-righteousness, and fear. Having one or all of these characteristics can make a genius resistant to change.

A leader of genius can change their focus to one that is more productive by using overt or subconscious methods. Overt methods include helping the genius visualize the purpose of the project and giving her ownership of the project. If you have a strong personal relationship with a genius, she might change her focus because you asked. If you have helped her in her own endeavors, she might reciprocate to help you in a new project. Finally, transferring authority for the new project to the genius may make her assume responsibility for the project, because you trust each other.

Once you have captured the interest of a genius, his mind is working long before you see any outward sign of his engagement with the problem. It might look as if he is still working on the previous project, but he will already be turning the new problem over in his mind. The reward for a genius's changing direction is his joy of discovery. That discovery must be intentionally marked and celebrated, so that he associates the reward with the change in direction.

To change the heart of a genius, you must understand and love the person for who he is. If you do not care about him, you will not be sensitive enough to entice him with the problem.

"Why can't we all just be professionals, and do what we get paid to do?" one of my former colleagues once said. Most employees can do that, but not a genius. The genius works for different reasons. If you do not understand those reasons, the genius on your team will underachieve or leave.

You can memorize the tools in this chapter, but if you do not care about the personal fulfillment of a genius, you will fail to change her direction. You will use a vision when the genius wanted a relationship. You will be withholding when you should have been generous.

Geniuses must jump off the cliff, fully committing to the project, to secure their best efforts and maximize their creativity. They can only do that if they believe in the purpose of the project. Give geniuses purpose before giving them the project.

CRUCIAL TAKE-AWAY

The first discovery of a genius in a new project should be the project itself.

RULE 10:
MAKE PEACE WITH CRISIS

12

eading genius means that crisis is a regular occurrence. Early on, Flexner met crises with a calm persistence that brought confidence to his faculty and to the nervous Bambergers. When he decided a genius was a good fit for the IAS, like Hermann Weyl, Flexner would not get upset if the genius initially turned him down. Even Einstein was difficult to recruit, wanting to split the IAS position with a position at the California Institute of Technology. The impact of Einstein's hiring would not have been nearly as great for the IAS if they shared him with another university.

When they were discussing this option, Flexner's letters to Einstein radiate calm and rationality. Flexner ultimately convinced Einstein to join the IAS full time with the promise that he could help decide which future faculty the IAS would hire. Flexner's quiet confidence attracted Einstein just as much as his vision for the IAS.

When George Birkhoff, the Harvard mathematician, reneged on their agreement, even though inwardly in turmoil, Flexner exuded calm to the Bamberger family and the rest of the IAS board. As mentioned, instead of retaliating against Birkhoff, he remained unperturbed and focused on recruiting Einstein, and his efforts paid off.

A short while after Einstein joined the IAS, he traveled back to Europe for a series of summer lectures held at Oxford and Paris. When Einstein's plans to leave Germany for the IAS were announced publicly, the Nazis confiscated his house and bank account containing 30,000 marks (about $220,000 currently). They even took his beloved violin. They expelled Einstein from the Bavarian Academy of Science. When Nazi youth burned a mountain of Jewish books in front of the Opera House, Einstein's works were among them.

Einstein's persecution made him internationally celebrated as a symbol of resistance to the Nazis. There was a rumor that the extreme German nationalist group Fehme offered $5,000 (more than $80,000 now) to anyone who would kill Einstein. While speaking at Oxford, Einstein was housed only ten miles from a large group of Nazis vacationing at a nearby resort.

Flexner was beside himself with anxiety over Einstein's safety. Many friends, including Flexner, urged him to return to the United States. Einstein refused, saying, "In these times of dire threats to Jews and liberals, one is morally obligated to undertake what one in normal times would avoid."[1]

Despite his inner turmoil during this time, Flexner maintained a supernatural calm. His calm gave the IAS the space it needed to grow during its infancy. Late in his tenure at the IAS, Flexner became irritable and angry in times of adversity. He attacked anyone opposing him and tried to browbeat the IAS faculty and board into supporting his decisions, on which he never asked for input.

Initially, most of the IAS faculty were highly supportive of Flexner. but they ultimately revolted against his leadership and asked the board to terminate him. Between Flexner's seeming tolerance of the anti-Semitism at Princeton and his dishonesty and unfairness over salaries, his faculty turned against him. Einstein found the tolerance of anti-Semitism especially offensive, as he personally had assisted in rescuing Jews from Hitler's Europe. For others, Flexner's perceived dishonesty and unfairness over faculty salaries were the problem. Even Edward Earle, whose job Flexner held open while Earle recovered from tuberculosis, turned against Flexner in the end. He wrote a letter to two board members asking for their support in forcing Flexner to resign.

The IAS board met urgently to consider the revolt of the IAS scientists against Flexner's leadership. Flexner had several supporters on the board, and they managed to delay forcing Flexner out as IAS director for a short while, as the board reviewed IAS finances. The board found the finances in a mess. Flexner had overcommitted significantly, to the extent that there were not enough funds to even cover current operating expenses.

Flexner did not handle the faculty revolt or the financial crisis well. He refused to take responsibility for either. He was outraged that his leadership was being questioned. His response was to pressure the IAS board to reaffirm his authority. He suggested that the board take principal from the endowment to fund the IAS operating deficit he had created. After a prolonged and bitter board meeting, he was unable to muster a majority of the board to support his request.

On October 29, 1939, the IAS board accepted Flexner's forced resignation. The *New York Times* covered the termination in lurid detail, giving the conflicts with the IAS geniuses as the main reason for his termination.

In the end, Flexner was a tragic leader of genius. He succeeded beyond anyone's dreams in building the IAS, but when he forgot the very reasons for his success, he crashed in spectacular fashion. If he could fail, so could any leader.

The Stress of Innovation

Technological innovation is always stressful, because it forces people to adapt when they were comfortable with the way things were. New technology forces them to admit that the way they had been doing things was not as good, which is close to being an indictment of individual inadequacy. This holds true inside organizations that rely on genius for advances.

"Great spirits have always found violent opposition from mediocrities. The latter cannot understand it when a man does not thoughtlessly submit to hereditary prejudices but honestly and courageously uses his intelligence," Einstein wrote.[2]

Since crisis is normal for leading genius, the final Rule is to make peace with crisis. Unless you can function normally during crisis, you will make poor decisions that will hurt the geniuses on your team. You will also transfer the stress of every crisis to the geniuses, which will crush their creativity. They will worry about the crisis instead of the project.

You need to exude calm even when you feel swept away by circumstances beyond your control. During my first cardiac arrest as a young physician training in the ICU, Dr. Mike Welsh said, "Take a deep breath. Think before you do anything. You have 240 seconds before the first neurons die."

Have you ever just sat in one place and watched the clock for 240 seconds? You cannot even concentrate on the clock, because it is such a long time. If there is no emergency, you get bored and your mind wanders. If you have this amount of time to make a decision during a cardiac arrest, then you should not have to force a rapid decision during a business crisis.

Crisis Can Blind You

Snap decisions imply that a wrong decision is acceptable, just because you are stressed. The time it takes to make a decision becomes the primary goal and not the outcome of the decision. Snap decisions are selfish, because you let your stress drive the rate of your decision making to move past the stressor. Calm lets you reject the tyranny of the urgent and broadens your options.

Crises blind you, because you focus on the timer of the bomb. You cannot stop focusing on what will happen when the bomb goes off. You start planning how to pick up all the body parts when you should be focusing on how to defuse the bomb. Crisis can make you focus more on the damage that might be done to your career than on how the crisis might harm the project or the team. If you find yourself worrying about what will happen to you if the crisis is overwhelming, then you no longer can make rational judgments. The heroes of a bomb squad are those who are still working on defusing the explosive even as it goes off. They focus so completely on the task that they never think about the consequences to their own person.

Calm in the face of crisis makes the Rules real. If you can stay calm in the face of a job-threatening crisis, you will show that you have inner principles, which will see your team through. This inner peace demonstrates strength of character that comes from knowing that the process by which you lead works. Without that inner peace, crisis can overwhelm your decision making.

Mirror Neurons

"Followers mirror a leader—literally," Daniel Goleman and Richard Boyatzis wrote.[3] Your team is the best measure of how you are doing as a leader. They will unconsciously mimic what they see. There is a neurological basis for the concept that you create the culture of your team by living it out yourself first. We all have cells in our brain called mirror neurons scattered throughout the frontal cortex, where most of our behavior is organized. These mirror neurons fire when you do something and when you see someone else do the same thing.

UCLA neuroscientist Marco Iacoboni proposed that these neurons help us discern the intentions of others from their current actions.[4] He said that these neurons are the basis for an empathic understanding between individuals. For example, he showed that mirror neurons could differentiate between someone picking up a teacup to drink from it or to clear it from the table.

When someone talking to you demonstrates sadness in the inflection of his voice or his body language, we tend to feel sad whether or not the words themselves are sad. We subconsciously detect the emotions and intentions behind the words someone is using and our mirror neurons reproduce the same emotions. This is why emotional intelligence is so important in a leader. You can destroy your message or you can enhance it by the way you deliver it.

Calm Creates Space

Perhaps the main reason to stay calm is to give yourself a few minutes to weigh which Rule applies, and then to implement that Rule. In a crisis, it is easy to react from an instinctual emotion before assessing which Rule applies to the situation. Calm prevents the tyranny of the urgent that drives rash decisions. Calm prevents the paralysis that comes from being hypnotized by the consequences of what could go wrong. Calm creates space in which your team can operate.

At the height of the Cold War in the 1960s, Soviet Russia tested a new intercontinental missile that could deliver nuclear warheads to far more American cities than before. A group of ballistic missile experts was secretly convened and told not to come out until they knew how to detect the new Soviet missile. The group was stressed and disjointed, because they hardly knew each other, and they felt the urgency of the situation.

"We did not even want to eat or go to bed," one of those missile engineers told me. The leader of that group knew that the underlying panic of those engineers would hurt their creativity.

The group's leader first had them get to know one another, talking about families and education. Then he had them step back and remove the problem from the context of Russia versus the United States in a nuclear war. Just thinking about the consequences of the problem was overwhelming. The leader made it an aeronautical engineering problem. Previously a professor at a university, he put the problem in theoretical terms, writing the equations out on an old chalkboard.

By creating relationships and putting the missile engineers in an environment with which they were familiar—being in a classroom and quizzed by a professor—he created the calm that gave them intellectual and emotional breathing space. In a few weeks, the scientists figured out how to detect these missiles and how they could be intercepted.

Calm allows you as a leader to create your own environment. It allows you to set the process for addressing the crisis and solving the problem. Calm shows that you believe in yourself. More than just believing, you know that the weight of your values is greater than the roar of the storm.

Calm Creates Trust

It is crucial that a crisis not change you. If external pressure can make you change your values, then you will lose the trust of your team, which can cripple their effort and enthusiasm. Holding to these Rules in crisis creates trust, because you become predictable. The genius you lead does not have to waste time guessing what you will do next or how you will behave. She or he knows that you will do the right thing for the right reasons no matter what. Teams cannot exist without trust.

If the team cannot trust what you say, they will think it is within the standards of the team to embellish the truth. Results will be fudged and data misinterpreted. In turn, you will begin to mistrust what your team says. Projects that looked initially as if they were highly innovative will come crashing down at the first real test, because the foundation upon which the project has been built is fissured with small untruths.

This is termed the amplification of faultfinding. If you as team leader tolerate the small, almost imperceptible mistakes and untruths, then as the project progresses the significance of these small cracks amplifies. These defects do not crack until there is a heavy weight on them. When these defects finally do crack, the project is already far along, and the crash causes more damage. This leads to the second characteristic of the amplification of fault.

The greater the crash, the more the finger pointing. The cost of the crash begs the question of whose fault it was. The cost of failure amplifies exponentially with the distance from the original defect.

The need to apportion blame also amplifies with the cost of failure. The need to apportion blame in a massive failure derives from a lack of trust within the team. Calm in the face of a failure prevents the amplification of fault and the need to apportion blame.

Calm Enhances Creativity

In 1989, an explosion in the middle engine of United Airlines Flight #232 severed all hydraulic lines leading to the wing flaps and tail rudder. There was no longer any way to direct the plane. The captain of that flight, Al Haines, furiously scanned the pilot's manual, but there was nothing in there that covered the situation.

They had only a few minutes before they stalled and spiraled into a crash. Flight recorders show that Haines and the copilot remained calm and even joked about having a beer together when they landed.

In that breathing space of calm, Haines came up with a brilliant idea. The only control he had was the throttle of the two remaining engines. By accelerating one side and decelerating the other, the differential thrust slowly turned the plane toward an emergency landing at Sioux City, Iowa. They slid sideways on the runway into a cornfield. Though 111 of the 282 passengers died from the ensuing fire, the fact that anyone survived at all is considered one of the greatest examples of a team responding to a crisis with calm and creativity.

"Maintaining our composure was one of the hardest things we had to do. We knew we had to focus and think straight," Haines said.[5]

Differential throttling of remaining engines is now standard technique for piloting disabled planes, but when Haines needed it, it did not exist. He invented it at that moment, for that moment.

Haines said he did not know where the concept of using differential thrust to turn the plane came from. He said, "I am no genius, but a crisis like that sure can sharpen the mind."[6]

Counting to 240

Calm in the midst of crisis prevents you from making decisions that are inconsistent with the Rules you want the team to live by. Calm enhances the confidence and creativity of your team.

When external stress translates into internal pressure to succeed, the chances that you will make a decision based on self-preservation rise. You cannot help it. The stress hormones cortisol and adrenaline force your brain to look out for itself.

The key to achieving calm in a crisis is to recognize that crises are normal. When pressured, we often rush to a decision, because the situation is uncomfortable. We want to get out of the stress as soon as possible as a pain avoidance mechanism. When you realize that external stress is the normal state of affairs for disruptive genius, you will find it easier to make peace with crises. You should set an internal buoy that rises or falls with your own internal stress. There are known biomarkers for stress, such as a rising voice, the blood rushing to the head, or a churning stomach.

When you feel that internal buoy rising, you need to step back and reset your brain. Never make a decision when that biological buoy is high. You will be making it for self-preservation and not for the ultimate good of the project.

I have several time-tested tricks I use when I feel overwhelmed and start breaking my own Rules. The stress hormones evolved to allow us to run away or fight. These hormones increase heart and breathing rate. Blood goes from the brain to the muscles, another reason we make bad decisions under stress.

The first thing I do when feeling stressed is physical activity, which uses the emergency energy the fight-or-flight response produces. I take a walk outside for a few minutes. I have done push-ups in my office. The first time I did this, my assistants thought I had lost my mind.

The next thing to do is eat a healthy snack. Though the brain runs on glucose, a pure sugar snack will result in high and then low blood glucose as insulin kicks in from your pancreas. If you want to avoid the low, you need a snack that has more complex carbs or protein than sugar.

For long-term internal stress, having a mentor to whom you can vent can restore you to calm. A mentor can help diffuse the feeling of impending doom by putting the crisis in its true perspective.

Hobbies also help relieve internal stress. Ken Kaushansky, vice president of SUNY Stony Brook, who works harder than anyone I know, loves model trains. One year my family was invited to his home for Thanksgiving. He showed me the new model train set-up he was working on, which filled his entire three-car garage with spectacularly detailed miniature mountains, people, and a town.

"It was a stressful year," he said when I asked him why he had built such a large train platform. "I enjoy it, and it gives me a few hours when I do not have to think about work."

Doing something you enjoy can create rest for your brain. It can distract your attention and give your brain peace. Just as resting between physical workouts allows your muscles to recover, taking a break refreshes your concentration and puts life into perspective. Dr. Cade enjoyed restoring vintage Studebaker cars. Paul Okunieff, a chair of Radiation Oncology at the University of Florida, who has started multiple biotech companies, kayaks the springs and mangrove swamps along the Florida coast.

There will always be external stress if you are trying to push the technological envelope. There will be competitors who want to beat you to market, there will be Luddites who oppose change, there will be pirates who steal your team's ideas, and there will be trolls who hoard resources. If you ever make a major advance, they will all turn on you and try to take it from you.

Self-Leadership

Staying calm when faced with a crisis is a learned skill. Everyone has the fight-or-flight surge of adrenaline when confronted with a crisis.

The key to staying calm is first to anchor yourself to the inner values the Rules represent. This is the best defense against the onslaught of stress that comes from leading genius. In addition, if you model calm for your team, they will mimic it through their mirror neurons.

We live in a results-driven society, and we often measure leadership by quantifying how many people you can get to follow your instructions. Leading genius, on the contrary, starts with grounding yourself in the values behind the Rules. Your belief in these values should be so strong that, no matter what the cost, you can be counted on to act a certain way.

Each of the Rules is based on an organizational value that all of us should believe in, no matter what the circumstances. Great leaders of genius measure success more by their adherence to these values than their own career advancement.

"Nothing so conclusively proves a man's ability to lead others as what he does from day to day to lead himself," wrote Thomas Watson, the founder of IBM.[7]

Values Anchor the Rules

Leading yourself starts with Rule 1, an understanding of who you really are. Unless you are continuously self-assessing, you will not know where you are weakest until a crisis. You can tell which areas of leadership you lack by the types of conflicts you avoid. Conflicts are often centered on a violation of a specific value.

You need to anchor yourself to values that you believe are more important than your job. Such principles are true even if you did not believe in them. If you value these principles more than you value your job, you will persistently apply the Rules during a crisis.

Many of us fool ourselves into thinking that we have a philosophy of leadership, but at the first crisis we compromise that philosophy as we rationalize our actions to ourselves. The values we really believe in are not the ones we espouse, but the ones we live during a crisis.

Without these internal values, the Rules will crumble during a crisis. The converse is also true. You can say you believe in these values, but if you do not implement the Rules during a crisis you are deceiving yourself. Implementing the Rules in times of stress demonstrates that you believe in the values behind the Rules. If these values are a part of your character, implementing the Rules will become easier and stress will not alter what you do.

Remember, you cannot hold one value without the others. They build on each other. If you do not value integrity, then it will be difficult for you to implement Rule 1. Integrity is being the same person internally and externally, in private and in public. Lie to yourself, and you will lie to others without even knowing it. Reality will be flexible, and you will bend it whenever it suits you. If you can be honest with yourself, you will have integrity in your relationships with others.

If you can see yourself as you really are using Rule 1, the unselfishness required for Rule 2 becomes easier. You know your limitations, and you know that hoarding power will result in less productivity for the team. Needing to be in control and at the center of every decision is selfish. You selfishly hoard power to build your own self-esteem. If your self-esteem is based on your ability not to be powerful but to be able to self-correct, then you can delegate power unselfishly.

If you are unselfish, it is easier to be humble, because your advancement is less important than the success of genius. Humility is the key to being able to listen to your team in Rule 3, because what a genius says becomes more important than what you could say.

Integrity, unselfishness, and humility lead directly to transparency, which is the value behind Rule 4. You will provide data and take the views of the genius into account before making a decision, because you know that the input will make the decision better. You will become accountable to the genius for your decisions, transparently reviewing each past decision in order to improve. If you lack integrity with yourself, you will by nature hide information and make decisions in secret.

Transparency leads to wisdom, the value behind Rule 5, because you learn from every decision by taking into account the views of the entire team. Every decision becomes an opportunity to learn, and the more you review each decision with the team, the more wisdom you gather.

When you gain wisdom, you realize that innovation can come from unexpected sources. If you are equitable, everyone has an equal chance at contributing, which is crucial for making breakthrough advances. Wisdom permits you to overcome the preexisting biases that limit your team's productivity. Without equity, the value behind Rule 6, your team will be anchored to its past.

Wisdom leads you to the value behind Rule 7, discretion. Discretion means that you wisely choose which actions to pursue. Discretion asks that you not say or do everything that comes to mind just because you can. Some words and deeds are harmful, and need to stay invisible.

Unselfishness, humility, and equity lead you to the value behind Rule 8, which is caring for your team. Caring means that you hurt when they hurt, and you rejoice when they rejoice.

You will consider each team member valuable, because each can contribute unique viewpoints and creative solutions. You will take into account subaltern viewpoints because every individual can have a stroke of genius. Equity and humility permit you to build nonlinear, flattened, hierarchical teams more easily.

Caring leads directly to the value behind Rule 9, respect. If leaders do not respect the geniuses they lead, they will force geniuses to work on a new assignment. Those leaders will not try to attract a genius with the new project. They will see that as a waste of time and issue concrete instructions instead. Their goal is not enhancing the creativity of the genius, but enforcing obedience.

It takes generosity with your time and effort to draw a genius toward a new project. Without respect and unselfishness, it would be impossible to implement Rule 9, which is to pull instead of push a genius in a new direction. The final Rule, keeping calm in the midst of a crisis cannot occur without courage. Courage is not just protecting the team in time of crisis, but it is also sticking to your values even when it costs you. This duty to values is not a popular stand, but it is crucial for leading genius. A genius will see right through your attempts at bending values to fit the situation. See Figure 12.1.

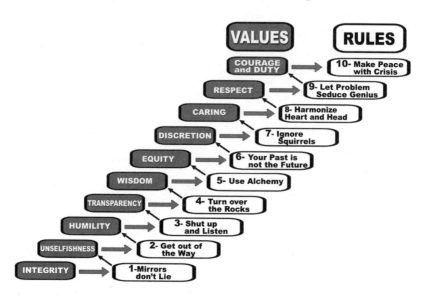

Only by having these values carved into your character can you use the Rules in times of crisis. These values anchor the Rules. Without them, you cannot implement the Rules when it is costly to do so. If you can implement the Rules when it is risky for your own career, you demonstrate that the success of the genius you lead is more important than your own success. At that point, a genius can stop worrying about success and begin to discover.

CRUCIAL TAKE-AWAY

During the storm of a crisis, first anchor yourself to your values.

SEEING OURSELVES IN ANOTHER

Let me suggest a single ethic that unifies all the values behind the Rules, which should be the single most important motivation for applying these Rules. The one foundational ethic behind the Rules is empathy—you recognize yourself in another.

You want geniuses to find the joy of discovery, because you want to share in that joy. You share in their hurts, because you want to share in their hopes and dreams as well. Though you may not understand the thought process of a genius, you can understand his joy.

Without empathy, without giving your team equal worth to yourself, you will refuse to be accountable for your actions. You will justify any harm you caused, because you will think that no one is as valuable as you are. You begin to believe that you are the reason the team exists.

When you fail to see yourself in another, you fall into an insidious trap. You will judge yourself by your intentions and not by what you actually did. You will judge others by their actions and not their intentions. You measure your virtue by what you meant to do, and you judge the virtue of others by their actions.

This disconnect between how we judge ourselves and how we judge others can lead to mutual mistrust. This makes everyone prone to overestimate his own virtue and underestimate the value of everyone else, especially in a crisis. I know that I forgive myself small mistruths, which generally make me look better in some fashion, but I am merciless about others being scrupulously correct.

Though we want to have values only when it is to our advantage and discard them in times of crisis, when it costs us to maintain them, we insist that everyone else keep them no matter what. By giving ourselves credit for feeling bad when we compromise, we create different psychological accounting between us and others.

Unless you can feel the hurt or joy another feels, you cannot be unselfish and humble. You will be less effective as a leader. You may not understand how the mind of a genius works, but you can gain insight into her or his heart. If you can for even a moment glimpse what is going on inside the hearts of those you lead, it is easier to make decisions on what is best for a genius. You become part of the team with the genius, as opposed to the genius becoming an extension of you.

Sharing both joy and suffering with the genius on your team means that you understand the reason why these Rules should be implemented. You want geniuses to reach that transformative breakthrough, so that they can experience the joy of discovery. You will share in the joy, and your greatest reward is a genius's success. By feeling joy for the genius who made a transcendent discovery, you become the genius yourself for a brief moment.

ACKNOWLEDGMENTS

This book is the result of many discussions over two decades with many leaders from multiple disciplines. Thomas Flannery was the agent and Diane Reverand the editor, both responsible for shepherding the book to publication. While those contributing to the Rules are too numerous to list here, we would like to acknowledge a number of leaders who have had the greatest impact. Major General Charles Scanlon, ret., U.S. Army, former director, U.S. Army Linguistics Program; Laney Whitlock, MBA, COO, and co-founder of BigTentCare.Com, former EVP of Federated Publishing; Edward Jimenez, MHA, CEO of Shands Teaching Hospital; Michael Boughton, Ph.D., former IT director for TRW Fluid Mechanics Group; John Kraft, Ph.D., dean of Warrington School of Business, University of Florida; Robert Thomas, J.D., Ph.D., chair of the Department of Management, Warrington School of Business; Burt Adelman, MD, former EVP of R&D at Dyax, former EVP R&D at Biogen; Cheryl Willman, MD, director and CEO of the University of New Mexico Cancer Center; Martha Liggett, J.D., executive director, American Society of Hematology; Edward Choi, MD, co-director, Jordan International Aid, and medical director, Palo Alto Homeless Shelter; Ken Kaushansky, MD, vice president for Health Sciences and dean of the School of Medicine, SUNY Stony Brook; Michael Caligiuri, MD, CEO of The James Cancer Hospital and Solove Research Institute and director of Ohio State's Comprehensive Cancer Center, and co-founder of Zivena and Arno Therapeutics; Jay Bradner, MD/Ph.D., now director of the Novartis Foundation and formerly associate professor of Harvard Medical School, co-founder of Acetylon, Shape, Tensha, and Syros; Pete Early, former *Washington Post* writer and best-selling author; David Vigliano, director of AGI Vigliano Literary LLC; Timothy Flynn, MD, former chief medical officer, UF Health; Les Hromas, Ph.D., program manager, Propulsion Laboratory, TRW/Northrup Grumman; Pope Moseley, MD, dean of the School of Medicine at the University of Arkansas; Fred Southwick, MD, Harvard University Advanced Leadership Fellow, and a medicine quality officer for University of Florida Health; David Guzick, MD/Ph.D., senior vice president for Health Affairs, University of Florida; Robert Leverence, MD, vice chair of the Department of Medicine at the University of Florida; Jon Licht, MD, director of the University of Florida Cancer Center; J. Larry Jameson, MD, dean of the Perelman School of Medicine at the University of Pennsylvania; Peter Buckley, MD, dean of the School of Medicine at Virginia Commonwealth University; Ethan Dmitrovsky, MD, provost at the University of Texas MD Anderson Cancer Center; Mark Anderson, MD/Ph.D., chair of Medicine at Johns Hopkins University; Mark Zeidel, MD, chair of Medicine at Beth Israel hospital at Harvard Medical School; Andrew Schafer, MD, former chair of Medicine at Weill Cornell School of Medicine; Hal Broxmeyer, Ph.D., former chair of Microbiology and Immunology at Indiana University; Steve DeKosky, MD, former dean at the University of Virginia School of Medicine; Steve Sugrue, Ph.D., senior associate dean for Research at the University of Florida; Kevin Behrns, MD, dean of the School of Medicine at St. Louis University; Scott Rivkees, MD, chair of Pediatrics at the University of Florida; Craig Brater, MD, director of the Alliance for Academic Internal Medicine and former dean of the School of Medicine at Indiana University; David Williams, MD, chief of Hematology-Oncology at Boston Children's Hospital; Bruce Blazar, MD/Ph.D., director of the Clinical and Translational Science Center at the University of Minnesota; Thomas Schwenk, MD, vice president and dean, University of Nevada Reno College of Medicine;

and Michael Good, MD, dean of the College of Medicine at the University of Florida.

The leadership team of the Department of Medicine at the University of Florida also played an integral role in this book: Rachel Palmer, MBA; Alicia Wood, MBA; Fay Yancey, MBA; Larry Edwards, MD; Ellen Zimmerman, MD, Carmen Allegra, MD; Mark Brantly, MD; Jamie Conti, MD; Mark Segal, MD/Ph.D.; Ken Cusi, MD; Mike Lauzardo, MD; West Reeves, MD; Chris Forsmark, MD; Marian Limacher, MD; Dave Nelson, MD; John Wingard, MD; Marc Zumberg, MD; Julia Close, MD; Richard Schofield, MD; and Brad Bender, MD. We appreciate Rachel Hromas for hosting us on weekends while writing the manuscript. Special thanks to Joshua Hromas for editing the manuscript and Eric Hilgenfeldt, MD, and Joshua Kramer, MD, for reading it.

REFERENCES

CHAPTER 1

1   Flexner, A. *An autobiography—A complete revision, brought up to date, of the author's I REMEMBER* (1940). Simon and Schuster, New York, NY. 1960. p. 45.

2   Clark, R. W. *Einstein: His Life and Times.* Harper Collins, New York, NY. 1972. p. 418.

3   Ericsson, K. A. et al. "The Role of Deliberate Practice in the Acquisition of Expert Performance." *Psychological Review* 100: 363–406, 1993.

4   Scialabba G. "Mindplay." *Harvard Magazine* 86:16, 1984.

5   Schumacher, E. F. "Small Is Beautiful." *The Radical Humanist* 37:18–22, 1973.

6   Simonton, D. *Scientific Genius.* Cambridge University Press, Cambridge, MA. 1988.

CHAPTER 2

1   http://www.cnn.com/2006/POLITICS/04/18/rumsfeld/

CHAPTER 3

1   Clark, R. W. *Einstein: His Life and Times.* Harper Collins, New York, NY. 1972. p. 739.

2   Ibid. p. 737.

3   https://www.youtube.com/watch?v=I1tKEvN3DF0

CHAPTER 4

1   Mullis, K. *Dancing Naked in the Mind Field.* Random House, New York, NY. 1998. p. 19.

CHAPTER 5

1   Deutsch, C. H. "At Kodak, Some Old Things Are New Again." *New York Times,* May 2, 2008. (http://www.nytimes.com/2008/05/02/technology/02kodak.html)

2   https://www.cnet.com/news/blockbuster-laughed-at-netflix-partnership-offer/

3   Nickerson, R. S. "How We Know—and Sometimes Misjudge—What Others Know: Imputing One's Own Knowledge to Others." *Psychological Bulletin* 125: 737-759, 1999.

4   https://www.forbes.com/sites/susanadams/2011/08/24/bosses-dont-listen-now-theres-proof/#5aebd53f29ee, from See, K. E., Morrison, E. W., Rothman, N. B., Soll, J. B. "The detrimental effects of power on confidence, advice taking,

and accuracy." *Organizational Behavior and Human Decision Processes* 116:272–285, 2011.

5 Tost, L. P., Gino F., Larrick, L. P. "When Power Makes Others Speechless: the Negative Impact of Leader Power on Team Performance." *Academy of Management Journal* 56: 1465–1486, 2013.

6 Galinsky, A. D., Rucker, D. D., Magee, J. C. "Power and perspective-taking: A critical examination." *Journal of Experimental Social Psychology* 67:91–92, 2016.

7 Hunsaker, P. L., Alessandra, A. J. *The Art of Managing People* (1998). Simon Schuster, New York.

CHAPTER 6

1 Collins, J. *Good to Great: Why Some Companies Make the Leap, and Others Don't* (2001). Harper Collins, New York. p. 72.

2 Nathan, O, Norden, H. *Einstein on Peace* (2017). Arcole Publishing, electronic edition, www.pp-publishing.com. Chapter 6.

3 *New York Times*, July 7, 1933, Albert Einstein Letter to the Editor

4 Mangalindan, JP. "LinkedIn CEO Jeff Weiner: Treat employees like adults, and you won't have leaks." *Fortune*, Feb 14, 2013. http://fortune.com/2013/02/14/linkedin-ceo-jeff-weiner-treat-employees-like-adults-and-you-wont-have-leaks/

5 Holton, GJ, Elkana, Y. *Albert Einstein: Historical and Cultural Perspectives* (1997). Dover Publications, Mineola, NY. p. 388.

6 Thompson, C. "The See-Through CEO." *Wired*, April 1, 2007. https://www.wired.com/2007/04/wired40-ceo/

7 Potters, JJM, Sefton, M, Vesterlund, L. "Leading-by-example and signaling in voluntary contribution games: an experimental study." *Economic Theory* 33: 169–182, 2007.

CHAPTER 7

1 Zee, A. *Einstein Gravity in a Nutshell* (2013). Princeton University Press, Princeton, NJ. p. XVIII.

2 Infeld, L. *Quest: An Autobiographical Account* (1980). AMS Chelsea Publishing, Providence, RI. p. 305.

3 Hackman, JR. *Leading Teams: Setting the Stage for Great Performances* (2002). Harvard Business School Publishing Company, Boston, MA.

4 Mungiu-Pippidi, A. "Good Governance Powers Innovation." *Nature* 518:295-297, 2015.

5 Losada, M, Heaphy, E. "The Role of Positivity and Connectivity in the Performance of Business Teams: A Nonlinear Dynamics Model." *American Behavioral Scientist* 47:740-765, 2004.

6 http://www.catalyst.org/system/files/why_diversity_matters_catalyst_0.pdf

CHAPTER 8

1 https://www.kaushik.net/avinash/seven-steps-to-creating-a-data-driven-decision-making-culture/

2   Nevins, M. *Abraham Flexner: A Flawed American* Icon (2010). iUniverse, New York, NY. p. 13.

3   Infeld, L. *Quest: An Autobiographical Account* (1980). AMS Chelsea Publishing, Providence, RI. p. 249.

4   https://www.gyro.com/onlyhuman/Only%20Human%20Executive%20 Summary.pdf

5   https://www.cio.com/article/2375671/leadership-management/even-data-driven-businesses-should-cultivate-intuition.html

6   Isaacson, W. *Einstein: His Life and Universe* (2007). Simon and Schuster, New York, NY. p. 448.

7   Schweber, SS. *Einstein and Oppenheimer: The Meaning of Genius* (2008). Harvard University Press, Cambridge, MA. p. 279.

8   Ibid, p. 34.

9   Ibid, p. 279.

10   Clark, R. *Einstein: The Life and Times*. p. 638.

11   Ibid, p. 639.

12   Bird, K, Sherwin MJ. *American Prometheus: The Triumph and Tragedy of J. Robert Oppenheimer* (2006). Vintage Books, New York, NY. p. 83.

13   Briefing presented by Gen Powell to the Outreach To America Program, SEARS Corporate Headquarters, Chicago, Illinois. http://www.au.af.mil/au/afri/aspj/apjinternational/apj-s/2011/2011-4/2011_4_02_powell_s_eng.pdf.

14   Clark, R. *Einstein: The Life and Times*. p. 651.

15   Tversky, A, Kahneman, D. "Belief in the Law of Small Numbers." *Psychological Bulletin* 76:105-110, 1971.

CHAPTER 9

1   Flexner, A. *The Usefulness of Useless Knowledge* (2017). Princeton University Press, Princeton, NJ. p. 81.

2   Ibid, p. 85.

3   http://www.businessinsider.com/jony-ive-this-is-the-most-important-thing-i-learned-from-steve-jobs-2014-10

4   Infeld, L. *Quest: An Autobiographical Account*. p. 293.

5   Clark, R. *Einstein: The Life and Times*. p. 645.

6   Ibid, p. 690.

7   Ibid, p. 690.

CHAPTER 10

1   https://www.ias.edu/hermann-weyl-life

2   Mark Segal, MD, chief of nephrology, University of Florida. Personal communication.

3   http://www.miamiherald.com/sports/college/sec/university-of-florida/article7239437.html

4   Panek, R. "The Year of Albert Einstein." *Smithsonian Magazine*, June, 2005.

5   *The Collected Papers of Albert Einstein*. Princeton University Press, Princeton, NJ. Volume 8, p. 234, doc. 238, July 21, 1916.

6   *The Collected Papers of Albert Einstein.* Volume 8, p. 230, doc. 233, July 14, 1916.
7   http://www.nbcnews.com/id/13804030/ns/technology_and_science-science/t/
     new-letters-shed-light-einsteins-love-life/#.WiQYBv6osr8
8   Isaacson, W. *Einstein: His Life and Universe.* p. 78.
9   Ibid, p. 83.
10   *The Collected Papers of Albert Einstein.* Volume 5, p. 46, doc. 67, December 11,
     1907.
11   Festinger, L, and Carlsmith, K. "Cognitive Consequences of Forced Compli-
     ance." *Journal of Abnormal and Social Psychology* 58: 203-210, 1959.

CHAPTER 11

1   Clark BW. *Eisenhower's Leadership: Executive Lessons from West Point to the
     White House* (2012). Shore Road Productions, LLC, Old Greenwich, CT. p. 46.
2   Bonner, TN. *Iconoclast: Abraham Flexner and a Life in Learning* (2002). Johns
     Hopkins University Press, Baltimore, MD. p. 234.
3   Clark, R. *Einstein: The Life and Times.* p. 540.
4   Abraham Flexner. *I Remember: The Autobiography of Abraham Flexner.* Simon &
     Schuster, New York, NY, 1940. p. 252.
5   Flexner, A. *The Usefulness of Useless Knowledge* (2017).
6   Gleick, J. *Isaac Newton* (2004). Vintage Books, New York, NY. p. 4.
7   Amabile, T., Kramer, S. "Talent, Passion, and the Creativity Maze." *Harvard
     Business Review* February 27, 2013. https://hbr.org/2012/02/talent-passion-
     and-the-creativ.
8   Isaacson, W. *Einstein: His Life and Universe.* p. 548.
9   Lepper, M., Greene, D., and Nisbett, R. "Undermining Children's Intrinsic
     Interest with Extrinsic Reward: A Test of the Overjustification Hypothesis."
     Journal of Personality and Social Psychology 28: 129-137, 1973.
10   Clark, R. *Einstein: The Life and Times.* p. 653.
11   Feynman, RP. *Perfectly Reasonable Deviations from the Beaten Path: The Letters of
     Richard P. Feynman* (2005). Basic Books, New York, NY. p. 396.

CHAPTER 12

1   Bonner, TN. *Iconoclast: Abraham Flexner and a Life in Learning.* p. 254.
2   Einstein letter to Morris Raphael Cohen, professor emeritus of philosophy at
     the College of the City of New York, defending the controversial appointment
     of Bertrand Russell to a teaching position, March 19, 1940.
3   https://hbr.org/2008/09/social-intelligence-and-the-biology-of-leadership.
4   Iacoboni M. "Imitation, empathy, and mirror neurons." *Annu Rev Psychol.*
     60:653-670, 2009.
5   Lehrer, J. *How We Decide* (2009). Houghton Mifflin Harcourt, Boston, MA.
     p. 128.
6   Ibid, p. 132.
7   Watson, T. Watson (1939) in: *American Druggist* 100: 40, 1939. https://en
     .wikiquote.org/wiki/Thomas_J._Watson

SOURCES

The major sources for events surrounding Einstein, Flexner, and the IAS were: Ronald Clark's superb *Einstein: His Life and Times*; Thomas Neville Bonner's fascinating *Iconoclast: Abraham Flexner and a Life in Learning*; Steve Batterson's insightful *Pursuit of Genius: Flexner, Einstein, and the Early Faculty at the Institute for Advanced Study*; Walter Isaacson's justly famous *Einstein: His Life and Universe*, and his *Einstein: The Life of a Genius*; Abraham Flexner's autobiography, co-authored by Allan Nevins, *Abraham Flexner: An Autobiography*; and Beatrice Stern's informative *A History of the Institute for Advanced Study: 1930–1950*. Einstein's own voluminous papers have been made publicly available by Princeton at http://einsteinpapers.press.princeton.edu/.

INDEX

ABOUT THE AUTHORS

ROBERT HROMAS, MD, MS, FACP

Robert Hromas is the dean of the Lozano Long School of Medicine at the University of Texas Health Center at San Antonio. In that role, he leads more than 1,300 faculty, 3,000 staff, and 800 physicians in training, with nearly $150 M in research expenditures. Prior to that, he was the chair of medicine at the University of Florida College of Medicine, where he was also vice president of the physician practice plan. He personally supervises a laboratory designing new cancer drugs and has published more than 160 academic papers. His research has been continuously funded by the National Institutes of Health for two decades. He was the chair of the Scientific Affairs Committee for the American Society of Hematology. He chaired multiple National Institutes of Health and American Cancer Society research review panels. He served as a scientific advisor for multiple pharmaceutical firms. He has been on several health care organization boards, including UF Health, a major health service provider with more than 10,000 employees. He won numerous teaching and patient care awards, including the Indiana University Humanism in Medical Education Award, Indiana University Board of Trustees Outstanding Teacher Award, and the People Living Through Cancer Caring Award. For these and other accomplishments, he was elected to the American Society of Clinical Investigation, the Association of Professors of Medicine, the American Clinical and Climatologic Association, and the Association of American Physicians.

CHRISTOPHER HROMAS, PH.D.

Christopher Hromas is a project manager at University of Florida Health. He received his Ph.D. and taught ethics and human nature at Fordham University. He has published multiple papers on ethics and has spoken internationally on this topic. He was an executive on the Fordham University Graduate Council, and past president of the Fordham Philosophy Society, for which he organized its annual conferences. He has a special interest in the relationship of genius to performance, discerning truth, and community.